Plants and Civilization

Third Edition

Biology books under the editorship of William A. Jensen, University of California, Berkeley

Biology, Kormondy, Sherman, Salisbury, Spratt, and McCain
Biology: The Foundations, Wolfe
Botany: An Ecological Approach, Jensen and Salisbury
Biology of the Cell, Wolfe
Plant Physiology, Second Edition, Salisbury and Ross
Plant Physiology Laboratory Manual, Ross
An Evolutionary Survey of the Plant Kingdom, Scagel et al.
Plant Diversity: An Evolutionary Approach, Scagel et al.
Plants and Civilization, Third Edition, Baker
Plants and the Ecosystem, Third Edition, Billings

Other books in the Wadsworth biology series

Biology: The Unity and Diversity of Life, Kirk, Taggart, and Starr
Living in the Environment: Concepts, Problems, and Alternatives, Miller
Replenish the Earth: A Primer in Human Ecology, Miller
Energy and Environment: Four Energy Crises, Miller
Oceanology: An Introduction, Ingmanson and Wallace

Plants and Civilization

Third Edition

Herbert G. Baker
University of California, Berkeley

Wadsworth Publishing Company, Inc.
Belmont, California

to Irene

Biology Editor: Jack Carey

Production Editor: Anne Kelly

© **1978 by Wadsworth Publishing Company, Inc.**

Printed in the United States of America

2 3 4 5 6 7 8 9 10 — 82 81 80 79

Library of Congress Cataloging in Publication Data

Baker, Herbert G
   Plants and civilization.

   Bibliography: p.
   Includes index.
   1. Plants and civilization. I. Title.
SB107.B3 1978   581.6   77-19097
ISBN 0-534-00575-6

Preface

This book is an introduction to the study of plants in relation to human beings. It illustrates the profound influence of plants on man's* economic, cultural, and political history, as well as the steps people have recently taken to improve chosen plants for their own purposes. Although the plants that will be used in the future may be different from those currently used, there is little doubt that people will continue for a very long time to be utterly dependent upon the solar energy stored by photosynthesis in plant materials. It thus remains vitally important that an appreciation of the human use of plants be widespread.

Indeed, as world population soars, wasteful methods of utilizing the photosynthetic bounty must be replaced by more conservative methods. The last chapter (Chapter 15) of this new edition of *Plants and Civilization* has been completely rewritten (for a second time) to emphasize how this challenge is being faced through improvements of conventional food-producing methods as well as through development of new methods of food production.

Considerable advances have taken place in a number of other areas of human contact with plants—notably in their use for drug production, in the domestication of neglected though potentially valuable plants, and in the breeding of new cereal crops that may go a long way to alleviate the food shortages that threaten the

*The word *man* in this book means *human being* or *humanity*. Except in a few places where the context makes the gender obvious, no distinction between male and female human beings is implied.

world. Our knowledge of the ancestry and history of the cereals (most particularly maize and wheat) has improved significantly since the second edition of this book was published. Consequently, Chapters 5 and 6 have been largely rewritten. Increasing biochemical information about the plants referred to is becoming available, and this is reflected where appropriate in the text; however, in a book of this size, details of plant structure and physiology cannot usually be given. Practically every page of this book has seen some updating or revision, incorporating the available new data. The list of suggested readings at the end has been thoroughly revised.

Plants and Civilization should be useful to students in a variety of fields—as a textbook in botany (at the introductory level as well as in more specialized classes dealing with "Plants and Human Beings"), and as background reading for geography, anthropology, other social science, and humanities courses. Because it demands only a rudimentary acquaintance with plant science, I believe this book will be useful as general reading for any university student. Most of all, I hope that *Plants and Civilization* is readable for itself, apart from any value which it may have as a textbook. It is my desire to play some part in developing an understanding and respect for our alliances with plants in the economy of nature, so that they may be fostered.

During the writing of this book, a number of persons have given unstintingly of their help. In particular, I wish to acknowledge the assistance of Ms. Susan Kreps, Mrs. Margaret Remerowski, and Mrs. Marian Spitzer for their work in typing the manuscript. The staff of the University of California Botanical Garden kindly facilitated my work in photographing specimen plants, and my wife was tireless in carrying out the photographic processing and, among other very helpful activities, compiling the index.

Contents

Contents

1

Plants and Prehistory

Preagricultural Uses of Plants

In this book we shall stress the point that civilization would have been impossible without agriculture. Consequently, we must begin by explaining our use of the latter term, which for our purposes means the tilling of land and the deliberate sowing or planting of crop plants. It may or may not be accompanied by the domestication of herdable animals. Clearly, such a complicated process as the practice of agriculture could not have arisen suddenly — it evolved. Before agriculture, people and their ancestors depended for food upon their activities as gatherers and hunters. During this earliest and longest period of human history, often called the Paleolithic or Old Stone Age, which began between one and two million years ago, there were at least four major advances of glacial ice over large parts of the Northern Hemisphere, and a purely food-gathering economy certainly lasted for several thousands of years after the ice had retreated. (In Europe this way of life persisted less than 10,000 years ago.) A state comparable with Paleolithic development in Europe continued in some regions of the world almost (or even) until the present day. For example, until the twentieth century there was enormous diversity to be seen in the way of life of North American Indians. Although many Indian tribes had relatively highly developed agricultural systems, making use of well-selected plants, others had practically none. In northern California, a gathering and hunting life was based on the gathering of shellfish, fishing, or the hunting of game, as well as on the making of mush from acorns, buckeye seeds, and other seeds—accompanied perhaps by the eating of berries and pine nuts. And yet, at the same time, agriculture—particularly that based on maize and sunflowers—had evolved farther east, and even in southern California.

Early Paleolithic man was able to eat berries for sugars and vitamins, nuts for oils, and grass seeds and various roots which furnished starches as a carbohydrate source; he depended on meat for most of his protein. As he left behind his apish ways, the first stage in the evolution of man's food habits appears to have been an increasing use of weapons for hunting and equipment for fishing. But then, well after he developed tool-making and learned to control fire for his own purposes, and even after he began to build houses and to provide himself with clothing from the skins of animals that he hunted, man concerned himself with agriculture.

The Origins of Agriculture

Until the present century, most ideas about the beginnings of agriculture were of European origin. This is not surprising, since much of the archaeological evidence has been found there and in the immediately adjacent areas of western Asia and North Africa. It seems likely, however, that during these million or so years, significant developments in man's history were also taking place in other parts of Africa and Asia, particularly in areas that were unaffected by the recurrent advances and retreats of the ice sheets. Indeed, there is evidence of relatively favorable circumstances for life in those areas of the tropics and subtropics that today are arid and inhospitable because, corresponding with the advances of polar ice in the north, there were pluvial periods in lower latitudes which produced conditions suitable for human existence.

It should be remembered also that the wanderers who entered North America from Asia and peopled the whole of the Americas were not agriculturists, but were nomadic hunters, with the dog as their companion. Agriculture developed here too, utilizing a number of plants not represented at all in Old World agriculture. Unfortunately, very little is known about the earliest agriculture in the New World. With a few notable exceptions (where caves were inhabited by groups of people), populations were probably too small and sparse to leave sufficient evidence for archaeologists before the foundation of civilized cities, remains of which are to be found, for example, in present-day Mexico, Guatemala, and Peru. By then agriculture was well developed.

Pressure upon emergent man to utilize plants for more than just a supply of fruits, seeds, and roots undoubtedly began earlier in colder regions than it did in the tropics. In the tropics, one may live unclothed and unsheltered and have little need for fuel-consuming fire. By contrast, in the later stages of the last glacial advance—perhaps 20,000 years ago—at least European man used fire to keep warm. Elsewhere, fire was certainly used much earlier. Having the use of fire, man was able to penetrate north into a chilly world. So, even at this early stage, man needed and used wood for fuel. After the retreat of the ice, wood from the newly abundant trees was used in making the framework for shelters.

Even though the higher apes make resting places out of branches in the forests, it seems likely that early man hunted most of his food animals in unforested areas where caves, in particular, would have been utilized for shelter. When houses began to be made they must have been constructed of rather flimsy and perishable materials, so that they could scarcely be expected to leave recognizable archaeological remains. Paleolithic rock paintings do show such houses, however, and give some clue to their nature. The oldest European wooden houses whose remains have been studied, date from the latter part of the Old Stone Age, and include the earliest of the famous Swiss lake dwellings.

There is much in common between the building of shelters such as these and the making of baskets. Wattle and daub house making is similar to the principle employed in basket making. Flexible branches, stems, or leaves are woven between upright poles forming walls, which are then smeared with clay on both sides. Roofs are constructed similarly. Both walls and baskets may contain reeds and rushes as well as pliable twigs. In the Sacramento Valley of California, Indians used tubular stems and leaves of the tule, *Scirpus acutus* (Cyperaceae), for this purpose; similar marsh-grown rushes, cattails, and reeds were utilized in other parts of the world. Thus, grasses and grasslike plants became important to man at an early time.

Human beings have long collected grass "seeds" (actually one-seeded fruits) for food, and grain from wild grasses is still harvested in the drier parts of tropical and subtropical areas of the world. Grasses were harvested in a different way in the Great Lakes region of North America by the Indians, who collected the grain of the aquatic "wild rice" (*Zizania aquatica*). In this case the grain was beaten off the plants into canoes as they were paddled among the plants. Wild rice has recently returned to culinary favor as a delicacy, and it is still collected from wild plants because its cultivation, which is also carried on now, presents many problems.

A notable feature of the wild grasses whose grain was collected is that their inflorescences shatter when the grain is ripe. This shattering or breaking up of the upper parts of the stem enables the fruits in the chaff to be dispersed separately—a vital matter for a wild plant. By contrast, modern cereal grasses have been selected for tougher stems that do not break up when the fruit is ripe; the grains, one from each flower, remain on the plant and can be harvested all together. Additional selection has provided us with races of many cereals—for example, wheat and barley—in which the grain or fruit can be threshed free from the chaff after the whole plant has been collected. Oats, however, still present us with difficulty in separating the chaff from the grain. An extreme condition of fruit retention is found in maize, where the whole grain-bearing cob (the inflorescence) is tightly wrapped in leaves; it will not fall off and must be picked. Quite obviously, maize is a highly modified food plant that has lost its original power of seed dispersal. Placing their growth and reproduction under human control is what is implied when plants are said to be "domesticated."

In ancient, preagricultural days, carelessness may sometimes have caused some of the collected grain from the wild grasses to be scattered around the habitation site, where it then germinated. It is likely that the ground near such a place of abode was particularly rich in nitrogen from rubbish and excreta, and, in this soil, seedlings then grew into especially luxuriant plants. This process might easily have suggested to early man the idea of deliberately sowing seed in order to produce high-yielding plants in proximity to his habitation. We now believe that agriculture, of which this is a primitive example, was invented independently in several separate regions, with southeast Asia, southwest Asia, northeastern Africa, and the mountainous areas of parts of the American continents as likely centers. It seems most likely that food production, rather than collection, began about 9000 B.C. in southwestern Asia, spreading from there through eastern Europe to the remainder of the latter continent. Pottery had not yet been invented. Nowhere was the introduction of agriculture sudden; in each region there was a prolonged period of "incipient cultivation."

The Paleolithic or Old Stone Age lasted longer in Europe than in southwest Asia. During this period there was no agriculture, but chipped stone tools and weapons were made. The period was succeeded by the Mesolithic or Middle Stone Age, which was a period of transition when agriculture may have begun; it lasted for several thousand years. Last came the Neolithic or New Stone Age, fully developed by 3000 B.C., in which polished stone tools became the rule and agriculture became well developed. Agriculture continued to expand, with the use of metals, up to the present day.

Developments in agriculture in other parts of the world probably followed a course similar to that in Europe and western Asia, although with different materials and in response to different stimuli. In Europe and parts of Asia, the melting of ice from glaciers in the mountains at the same time as the onset of the Mesolithic Age (roughly 8000 B.C.) may have provided an abundance of aquatic habitats and good fishing. This, in turn, would have led to the formation of communities of people that stayed in one place for protracted periods, an essential precondition for the development of agriculture.

Rubbish piles rich in organic nitrogen would have come into existence around these fishing communities. Many of the plants that we believe were cultivated by early man are *nitrophiles,* which reach their most luxuriant development where this element is abundantly available. Hemp (*Cannabis sativa* —

Fig. 1-1) is such a plant. This and other nitrogen-loving plants are especially likely to grow as weeds in rubbish piles, a circumstance that could have led to their eventual cultivation.

Figure 1-1. A portion of a hemp plant (*Cannabis sativa*) showing pistillate inflorescences. From an herbarium specimen, University of California Herbarium.

In other cases, it is suggested that the first settlements were made in places where desirable food plants grew naturally (probably in moist soil) and could be collected easily. Growth of the human population would ultimately pressure people to move away from the area of abundant food plants onto "marginal lands." Here, wild plants would be neither abundant nor naturally luxuriant, and a stimulus would be felt to increase the yields from desirable kinds by clearing away competitors (they would be called "weeds"). Fertilizing the soil by burning the natural vegetation and sowing crop plant seeds would be logical developments. Thus, agriculture would develop. Semi-arid regions are likely starting places for this kind of agriculture because, compared to moist, forested areas, the land is easier for people provided only with stone tools to weed and clear by burning.

Multipurpose Plants

An important feature of the early cultivated plants is that they have many uses. Hemp can be used as a fiber plant or as a drug plant; in addition, a useful oil can be obtained from its seeds.

Some of the best examples of multipurpose plants are trees. The baobab tree, *Adansonia digitata* (Bombacaceae — Fig. 1-2), in the savanna regions of Africa, while not so much cultivated as protected, has long been put to many uses. Rope can be made from its bark; its leaves can be dried and used as medicine or to thicken stews. The fruits contain seeds that are a rich source of oil, and the pulp in which they are embedded has long provided Africans with a refreshing drink containing tartaric and other acids (Fig. 1-3). (It was not realized until recently that this pulp is also an excellent source of vitamin C.) Even the hollowed-out trunks of old baobab trees have their uses. They can be used to hold water (a precious commodity in the savanna regions

Figure 1-2. A baobab tree (*Adansonia digitata*) by a roadside in northern Ghana, West Africa.

Figure 1-3. Fruits of baobab (*Adansonia digitata*) on sale in a market in northern Ghana, West Africa. In the basket is white pulp from the interior of the fruits.

where these trees grow) or for the dry storage of materials. And in these lands where it is difficult to bury corpses in hard ground during the dry season, the dead may be allowed to mummify inside a baobab trunk.

In China, the mulberry tree, *Morus alba* (Moraceae), which has been used since antiquity, grows around villages. It is also a multipurpose plant; the fruit is excellent for human consumption and the leaves are food for silkworms. Its wood is valuable, and a yellow dye can be extracted from its roots.

Another example of a multipurpose plant, to be discussed in more detail later, is the coconut palm, which, for coastal peoples throughout the tropics, is an almost universal provider. In Mexico, several species of the genus *Agave* are renowned as having "a thousand uses" (Figs. 1-4 and 1-5).

Figure 1-4. *Agave sisalana*, a native of Mexico, used for a multitude of purposes. Rope-making fibers are obtained from the leaves, and sap from the stalk of the big inflorescence (not shown here) may be fermented to produce pulque. A row of plants makes an impenetrable "living fence." Growing at University of California Botanical Garden.

Generally, however, we may assume that plants whose primary value is as food were those to which attention was given first. Man can go naked in the tropics and can wear animal skins in colder regions; there is no place in the world where he can do without food.

Root Crops and Cereal Crops

Another suggestion that has been made is that the first deliberate growing of food plants was probably the planting of "root crops," wherein man makes use of the food-storing underground parts of plants. In some cases these are true roots; in other cases they are modified stems. In all cases they are rich sources of carbohydrates. It has been suggested, with very little evidence, that root crops were probably first cultivated in humid southern Asia between 13000 and 9000 B.C.

The use of roots is a simple form of agriculture. The plants can be dug up with a simple digging stick, the root or underground stem eaten, and any surplus returned to the soil. For this reason, root crops can be used by peoples who are not yet fully settled in villages. These people can dig up the roots, eat what they need, replant the remainder, and return a year or two later to find the roots increased in amount. The taro, *Colocasia esculenta* (Araceae), is perhaps one of the best known examples of such an Asian root-crop plant. In this plant, and in the extremely similar West Indian tania (*Xanthosoma sagittifolium,* Fig. 1-6), the underground portion is a *corm*—a short, swollen stem covered with fibrous leaf bases (Fig. 1-7).

David Harris has suggested that actual cultivation of root crops began with the weeding out of less useful plants from natural communities to allow more room for the desired plants. This was followed by the realization that the crop "roots" could be planted and would thrive in comparable habitats not already containing them if these, too, were weeded.

Although the first development of agriculture may have involved plants with food-storing underground parts, it is certain that the development of cereals also came at a very early stage, and it is a significant fact that we know of no important civilization that was not based on some kind of cereal. Cereals have many advantages as food plants, even apart from their high yield per

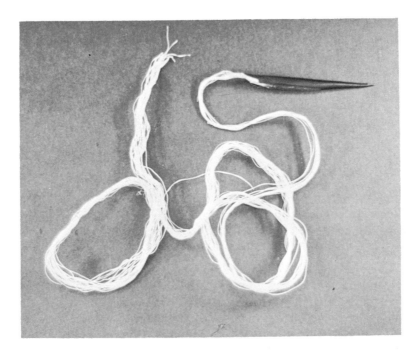

Figure 1-5. "Needle and thread" made in Mexico from the spine that tips an agave leaf and the fibers that run through the leaf. They are made by pulling the partially severed spine out of the rest of the leaf. Courtesy of Mrs. Erich Thomsen.

Figure 1-6. A plant of tania (*Xanthosoma sagittifolium*). Grown at University of California Botanical Garden.

acre. Their grains—one-seeded fruits—are compact and dry, and so they store well. They contain carbohydrates, fats, proteins, minerals, and vitamins, and thus truly can be called the staff of life. The straw from the cereal plants can be used for baskets and bedding, and for the construction of houses. Root crops, by contrast, though rich in carbohydrates, are generally less rich in other food substances.

The yield of cereal plants is increased by their habit of tillering, or producing lateral, flowering shoots from the axils of the lowest leaves on the stem. Because of this characteristic, young cereal plants may be grazed by domesticated animals, a practice that actually promotes more tillering. After grazing, the tillers may be allowed to grow up to produce their harvestable grain.

In at least one area of the world where cereal growing is not possible—the higher Andes of South America, above the maize-growing zones—a method of dehydrating root crops by freeze-drying in the snow was developed. Here, the Indians still produce *chuños* by dehydrating "Irish" potatoes and oca tubers—*Oxalis tuberosa* (Oxalidaceae—Fig. 1-8). The expression of the juices from the latter as part of the drying process is necessary to get rid of the toxic oxalic acid, which characterizes the genus.

Cereals appear to have developed usually in or near mountainous regions

Figure 1-7. A taro corm—the short, swollen underground stem produced by *Colocasia esculenta*—which forms a very important source of starch for people living in the wetter tropical regions. In southeast Asia, these may have been among the first crop plants deliberately planted.

of the subtropics and tropics. The small-seeded cereals belonging to such genera as *Panicum* and *Pennisetum* (Fig. 1-9), which are lumped together under the name "millets," were possibly the first to be used. Later, larger grains appear to have been developed in Ethiopia (Abyssinia), southeast and southwest Asia, southeastern Europe, and the Americas.

The antiquity of cereals is attested by the discovery of wheat grains in archaeological remains from a village in Iran that is believed to have been in existence over 9,000 years ago.

The contribution of the American continent to our roster of cereals is maize, which may have developed on the Amazonian side of the Andes or, more likely, in Mexico. Rice, a tropical and subtropical plant from the hills and low-lands of Asia, is the exception to the montane development of cereal plants (Figs. 1-10, 1-11, 1-12, and 1-13).

Although mountain regions may have seen the origins of cereal agriculture, the later development of irrigation techniques on the lower slopes would have enabled these crops to spread down and away from the mountains. Only then was it possible for the civilizations that appeared in the valleys of the Indus, Tigris, Euphrates, and Nile rivers to develop. Assyrian and Babylonian irrigation

Figure 1-8. Leaves and two plants of Oca (*Oxalis tuberosa*). At the bottom are a fresh tuber (right) and one dried into a chuño (left).

systems were particularly impressive, utilizing canals lined with bricks held together with tar, and it has been estimated that in 1800 B.C. they watered an agricultural area of 10,000 square miles.

Cereals provide excellent food, but, unlike the root crops, they demand a truly sedentary population. Generally they can be sown and reaped only at definite times of the year and will not last if they are left beyond the time for harvesting (as the root crops will). Nevertheless, the high-yielding, storable nutritious crop they provide offers the possibility of some measure of relaxation to a cereal-growing community. There is time for education and the transmission of knowledge and, therefore, for progress in civilization.

In the Asian tropics, the cereal that most obviously promoted the development of civilization was rice; in its absence, large and concentrated populations have not developed. More than half of the world's population depends heavily upon rice for sustenance—in Central and South America now, as well as in Asia. Two species are cultivated: *Oryza glaberrima* in West Africa, and *O.*

sativa, the common rice of the rest of the world, which may be derived from the wild perennial rice of India, *O. perennis.* Two groups of varieties exist within *O. sativa* — the so-called "indicas" and "japonicas" (see Chapter 15). The two groups cannot be intercrossed easily, so they have probably been separate since early in the history of rice cultivation.

Most rice in Asia is "paddy rice," grown in standing water until the time of harvesting (Figs. 1-11, 1-12, and 1-13). Where abundant irrigation water or the necessary engineering technology is not available, "upland rice" varieties, which depend on natural rainfall, are grown. This is the case in the American tropics (with the notable exception of recent large-scale Amazonian developments). Paddy rice gives a higher yield and, if plants can be raised in a seed bed and later transplanted into the fields (Fig. 1-12), up to three crops per year can be obtained in wet tropical regions.

In the twentieth century, highly mechanized rice cultivation (using airplanes to sow the pregerminated seed and spread fertilizers and pesticides) has developed, particularly in the Sacramento Valley of California.

In dry, tropical regions with land unsuitable for the intensive cultivation of high-yielding rice, shifting cultivation with substitute plants such as root crops, some cereals, and bananas has been necessary. Shifting cultivation involves

Figure 1-9.   Pearl millet (*Pennisetum typhoideum*) on the left and proso millet (*Panicum miliaceum*) on the right. From pressed specimens. Compared with wheat or maize, the grains are small.

clearing part of a forest or savanna, using the fertile soil built up under the natural vegetation for two or three years, and then, as the soil becomes exhausted, ceasing cultivation and allowing the land to return to its natural condition while another area is cleared and farmed. Sometimes as much as twenty years must elapse before soil fertility is restored and the same land can be used again. Clearly this situation does not favor the buildup of large, sedentary populations.

Figure 1-10. Three heads of rice (*Oryza sativa*) in nearly ripe condition. Grown at University of California Botanical Garden.

Sorghum (Fig. 1-14) and millets are grown, often in a shifting cultivation, in Africa, and as much use as possible is made of these plants. Not only do they serve as producers of grain (and, from this, of beer), but their straw is used for the making of baskets as well as for the construction of walls and roofs of houses. Even the poorer cereals, then, are extremely important crop plants.

We shall speak later (Chapter 2) of Nicolai Vavilov's contribution to our knowledge of the history of economic plants. Nevertheless, we should mention here one important distinction that he made in his studies: the separation of

Figure 1-11. Rice "paddies" in Java, built by terracing. The crop is grown in the flooded fields. Photograph courtesy of United Nations, F.A.O.

Figure 1-12. Gathering rice seedlings from the thickly sown seedbed for transplantation to the rice fields or "paddies." Thailand. Photograph courtesy of United Nations, F.A.O.

Figure 1-13. Indonesian woman cutting rice in Java. The paddies are drained before harvest. Photograph courtesy of United Nations, F.A.O.

Figure 1-14. Inflorescence of sorghum (*Sorghum bicolor*).

primary crop plants from those that could be classed as secondary. Secondary crop plants are those that have developed from weeds growing among the primary crop plants (Fig. 1-15). Thus, as wheat was carried northward over Europe with the spread of Neolithic agriculture from the Mediterranean region,

Figure 1-15. Left to right: a comparison of "heads" (inflorescences) of oats (*Avena sativa*), barley (*Hordeum vulgare*), a "beardless" bread wheat (*Triticum aestivum*), and rye (*Secale cereale*). Barley and wheat are primary crop plants; oats and rye are secondary.

rye (*Secale cereale*) or its ancestor was also carried along as a weed. In northern regions, because of its ability to start growth at lower temperatures than wheat, it grew taller and out-yielded the wheat crop. As a consequence, rye was selected as the cereal crop plant there. Today, its cultivation extends to within the Arctic Circle. A similar story probably applies to oats (*Avena sativa*), which may have begun its association with man as a weed of other cereal crops. As a species, it is tolerant of a wide variety of climates.

In conclusion, we should pay respect to the contributions of ancient human cultivators to the history of our economic plants. It is a striking thought that, although modern agriculture has improved the yields of crop plants, practically no new species have been introduced to cultivation within historical times. Almost all the food and fiber plants that we value today were known to the early agriculturists in the Old or New World. Many of them are so altered that their wild ancestors cannot be traced with certainty, and some are so old that they seem to have no wild relatives still living. Even among the drug plants — the group of economic plants that have attracted much attention in recent years as sources of reserpine, curare, and other twentieth-century drugs — are plants that have long been used in those areas of the world where they grow wild. Often they were not used for their modern, sophisticated purposes; their utility lay in their contributions to religious ceremonies, to witch-doctoring, and to making war. But even untutored early man had found at least some of their value.

2

Plants and History

Greek Pioneers in Botany

Although human beings domesticated plants at an early date, they probably did not study them closely for a long time afterwards. Occasional plant sketches, made for example, on horn by Paleolithic artists, exist, but they are not nearly so common as pictures of animals, and it seems clear that people were inclined to take the plants in their environment much more for granted.

Botanical science, the *study* of plants rather than simply their utilization, appears to be quite recent, having its roots in the culture of ancient Greece, although a papyrus from Egypt, estimated to date from 1600 B.C., contains a list of drug plants and their uses, and Assyrian contributions to the subject (700 B.C.) are known.

Earlier people probably had to live, of necessity, a very practical life. After all, one cannot be a philosopher until one has a certain measure of security and relaxation from the mere business of making a living. Even with the Greeks, botany appears as a study of medicinals earlier than in any other form, and Hippocrates and others wrote important works on this subject between 460 and 370 B.C.

The real beginnings of botanical science, however, appear to lie in the work of Aristotle (384–322 B.C.) and Theophrastus (370–287 B.C.), both of whom were pupils of Plato. Unfortunately, only fragments of Aristotle's botanical works remain, and we must depend more upon his pupil and colleague Theophrastus, sometimes called the father of botany.

Born on Lesbos, an island off the coast of what is now Turkey, Theophrastus succeeded Aristotle as head of the Lyceum in Athens. As such, he inherited Aristotle's garden, which contained about 450 species and was the earliest botanical garden of which we have any knowledge.

Theophrastus wrote two important books containing a number of seemingly modern ideas. For example, he indicated the essential differences between monocotyledonous and dicotyledonous plants, and he was aware of the basis of annual ring formation in woody plants. Also, he distinguished between the flower heads of what we now call the Compositae and the individual flowers of other kinds of plants. In addition, he was, in his way, an ecologist, for he described the communities of plants to be found in grasslands, woodlands, and marshes. Of course he also made a list of drug plants, some of which he had learned about during his experiences with the armies of Alexander the Great. However, although Theophrastus may have been the father of general botany, he seems to have had no real descendants for about 18 centuries.

Herbals

After the death of Alexander the Great in 323 B.C. and the breakup of his empire, Alexandria became the scientific center of the world for about three centuries. Then Rome took over, and little scientific progress was made in botany even though the Romans were good practical agriculturists. Pliny the Elder (23–79 A.D.) made a compendium of facts about living plants and animals, but it was very inaccurate.

However, one person of real importance in botany who lived during the Roman period was the physician Dioscorides. He was born about 64 A.D. and traveled widely, mostly in service as an army surgeon under the Emperor Nero. Dioscorides wrote one of the earliest herbals. An herbal is a listing, with illustrations, of plants and their properties, emphasizing medicinal aspects. Historically, Dioscorides' *De Materia Medica* was the most important of these productions. In it he described and illustrated about 500 medicinal plants. This manuscript was laboriously copied and recopied during the next 15 or 16 centuries, during which it formed the basis of most of the botanical works that were written. In fact, the book exerted so much influence during this period that there was great difficulty in getting any plant accepted for its medicinal value if it had not already been recommended by Dioscorides.

After the introduction of printing into Europe in the fifteenth century, herbals began to appear in profusion, even though many of them were simply plagia-

Figure 2-1. Leonhart Fuchs. From *De Historia Stirpium Commentarii Insignes*, 1542.

risms of the original herbal by Dioscorides. Nevertheless, in the sixteenth century, botanical science began to revive. Several herbals of considerable merit were produced, such as those published in 1542 by Leonhart Fuchs (Fig. 2-1), after whom the genus *Fuchsia* is named, and in 1576 by L'Obel, whose name in latinized form was Lobelius and after whom the genus *Lobelia* is called. *De Historia Plantarum* by Valerius Cordus, published in Prussia in 1561, was another milestone. Although these works were great improvements over earlier ones, they still propagated many myths. Particularly striking was the myth of the mandrake. It is true that there is a grain of truth in most myths, and, as we shall see, there was truth in some of the assumed wonderful propties of the mandrake plant. Nevertheless, the picture was almost comically overdrawn.

Mandrake — Myth and Reality

The mandrake, *Mandragora officinarum*, an herb of the tomato family, the Solanaceae, has a fleshy root that is often forked, particularly when, in growing down through the soil, it encounters a stone. The root of such a plant, when removed from the soil, might bear a vague resemblance to the torso and lower limbs of a human figure (Fig. 2-2). In those days it was believed that the ap-

---

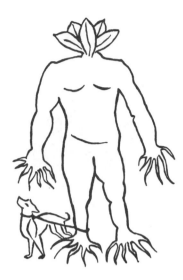

Figure 2-2. Mandrake (*Mandragora officinarum*). Fanciful representation of the herb being drawn from the ground by a dog. From the *Herbarium Apuleii Platonici*, c. 1481.

pearance of a plant was very often a guide to its utility, the sign being placed there by the Creator. This doctrine of signs, or doctrine of signatures, therefore, suggested that, because it resembled a human figure, the mandrake would be an efficacious plant to use in the treatment of human disease.

The mandrake was not common as a wild plant, nor was it easy to grow, and this added to its assumed value. In all probability, it was in order to protect it from indiscriminate use, and therefore extermination, that a myth was allowed to evolve concerning the supposed danger of digging this plant from the ground. It was suggested that anyone who did so would hear a death-dealing shriek as the plant was pulled up. Needless to say, very few people were willing to risk this fate, and ingenious methods of extracting the plant from its natural environment were devised. The favorite method, repeatedly illustrated in herbals, was to unearth the plant partially and then tie a string around the basal rosette of leaves, fastening the other end of the string to the neck of a dog. The dog was then incited to pull and be the agent of removal of the mandrake from the ground (see Fig. 2-2). The onlookers, by stuffing their ears with wool, were saved from hearing the lethal shriek.

What was it about the mandrake that made it worthwhile going to so much trouble and taking so much risk to harvest it? From ancient times, this plant has had a reputation for producing sleep, and its use probably constituted the first anesthesia. If the root were boiled or soaked in wine, a draft of this concoction could be given before a surgical operation and, supposedly at least, the pain would be dulled. However, this was a powerful drug, and it was recognized that too much mandrake brought on mental disease or even death. It has been suggested that mandrake was in the wine offered on a sponge to Christ on the cross, for its use in Roman times is well authenticated.

Mandrake root was analyzed chemically in 1889 and was found to contain a mixture of pain-deadening alkaloids, the most effective of these being hyoscine or scopolamine.

Mixed with morphine (from *Papaver somniferum*), this drug has been used to produce "twilight sleep," useful in easing the pain of childbirth and in other situations where the cooperation of the patient with the doctor is needed. Nowadays, more abundant sources of scopolamine have been found, and barbiturates have replaced the use of these alkaloids for many medical purposes.

This situation is one that has been repeated numerous times in history. Without understanding the means of action of a particular plant, man discovers that the principle present in it is of value in the treatment of some human condition. Many years later an analysis is made and the chemical nature of the active principle is discovered. Then it is synthesized — but even that is not the end of the story, for often, subsequently, an even better drug for the purpose is manufactured.

Scopolamine, it may be added, is also found in the leaves of shrubs of the genus *Duboisia* (also of the Solanaceae). These leaves have been chewed by Australian aborigines for relief from fatigue, hunger, and thirst since long before the European discovery of their country. Pituri, as the drug is called in this case, was also used by them to poison fish and to stupefy (for easy capture) the emu, which came to drink at the water holes. Here is a remarkable example of the independent discovery of similar important properties of plants by primitive peoples.

Botany and Botanical Gardens

Late in the sixteenth century, plants again began to be examined, and there were attempts at botanical classification, including the classification of useless as well as useful plants. It is not our purpose to follow the progress of botanical classification, but it is very relevant to point to the fact that many plant classifiers and writers of herbals were also directors of botanical gardens, which, in those days, were primarily medicinal or physic gardens (Fig. 2-3).

The oldest extant botanical garden is one of this kind, being that of the Vatican, founded in 1227, but not now occupying its original site. Several of the sixteenth-century Italian gardens still exist in their original locations, such as the garden at Pisa, founded in 1543, and the slightly younger gardens at Padua and Florence, all of which are still operative. In England, the Elizabethan Age (1533–1603) appears to have been a time of plentiful introduction of

Figure 2-3. The Physic Garden of the Society of Apothecaries, London (The Chelsea Physic Garden), as it was in 1750. Reproduced from an engraving at the Garden, by permission.

plants into gardens; one estimate is that over a hundred species were added to the list of medicinal herbs of foreign origin.

These physic gardens gradually developed into the modern European botanical gardens, their growth being the greatest in the eighteenth and nineteenth centuries as rapidly growing explorations in remote parts of the world produced an increasing flow of plant imports. The year 1789, for example, saw the introduction to London of *Rosa chinensis*, a parent of our modern roses, and *Chrysanthemum indicum*, the ancestor of the cultivated chrysanthemums of the autumnal flower garden. Not only were new plants brought in from other countries, but new horticultural forms were developed in European countries themselves. By the nineteenth century, a respectable botanical garden could not have just a chrysanthemum; it had to develop and present a selection of the best chrysanthemums.

In addition, although botanical gardens had for some time fulfilled an educational role in relation to medicine, as plant science came to be taught in the universities the gardens began to give instruction to students of botany and also to the general public. Botanical gardens also began to employ experimenters who engaged in plant breeding, and to sponsor expeditions to the less well-explored parts of the world to find new botanical treasures.

In the New World the development of botanical gardens followed a rather different pattern from that to be seen in Europe. A few American gardens began as physic gardens, but most of them are too modern for that kind of history.

Usually they have had their origin in gifts or bequests of their estates by wealthy men. For example, the famous 75-acre Missouri Botanical Garden in St. Louis (Fig. 2-4), was given to the public in 1889 by Mr. Henry Shaw, a St. Louis merchant, who had developed the garden for approximately 30 years. It became famous for its water lily displays, its orchid collections, and its shows of cultivated plants, particularly chrysanthemums; but it also possesses a fine library and herbarium. Most recently there has been developed at the Missouri Botanical Garden the most advanced display greenhouse to be seen anywhere. This is the famous "Climatron," where, under a single geodesic dome and without cross walls, several quite different climatic regimes are maintained for the proper display of the plants needing such conditions. Research is carried on in association with Washington University, and the garden is the source of a number of botanical journals.

The development of the Missouri Botanical Garden illustrates several general points, the first of which is the development in the nineteenth and twentieth centuries of herbaria in connection with gardens. Although gardens came first, it was soon found that the plants in the collections could not be kept growing indefinitely. Plants become old and may die; sometimes they will not reproduce in the artificial conditions of the garden, where they may also be subject to the lethal effects of frosts, gales, over-watering, and disease. Consequently, to maintain a record of the appearance of parts of those plants that may have

Figure 2-4.   View of the lily pond and the "Climatron" display greenhouse at the Missouri Botanical Garden, St. Louis. Courtesy of the Garden.

---

been growing in the garden or were collected in nature, it is necessary to preserve them. This is most easily effected by drying parts of the plant under pressure to produce the familiar herbarium specimen. In this way, a collection of specimens may be assembled which requires relatively little storage space, and these specimens are conveniently available for study and comparison at all times of the year. Some of the largest herbaria and plant museums in the world are in botanical gardens.

The second point is that there is a tendency in modern times not just to collect plants but to experiment with them, so that they and scientific problems associated with them may be better understood. Here, an important role has been played by botanical gardens that are associated with universities.

In the second half of the twentieth century we are witnessing a new tendency in the development of botanical gardens. Instead of gardens and experimental stations being established in temperate regions and plants being brought to them from the tropics, gardens are being established in increasing numbers in tropical regions. Even though many old public gardens that played a significant role in the development of colonial empires (see Chapter 11) have fallen on hard times, the foundation of new gardens is accompanying the continual development of new universities in tropical countries. This trend holds very great promise for the future of botanical research, for many of the outstanding problems in plant morphology, physiology, and evolution will be more easily solved when they can be tackled in the cradle of flowering-plant evolution, the tropics.

Studies of the Origins of Cultivated Plants

The classic work on the origins and histories of economic plants is *L'Origine des Plantes Cultivées*, published in 1883 by the great Swiss botanist Alphonse de Candolle. It has been translated into English and other languages. De Candolle's main conclusions regarding the domestication of cultivated plants are still largely accepted, although his datings of events are generally far too recent.

De Candolle used historical writings (including biblical sources as well as travelers' accounts), archaeological and ethnological data, and philology (linguistics) in determining the origins and travels of cultivated plants. He attached special significance to the presence of wild relatives in determining the place of origin of a cultivated plant.

More modern criteria have been added by the Russian agriculturist Nicolai Vavilov. He published a major work in 1926 on the centers of origin of cultivated plants, and in this he used information from genetics, chromosome studies, and anatomical investigations. One of his important theses was that

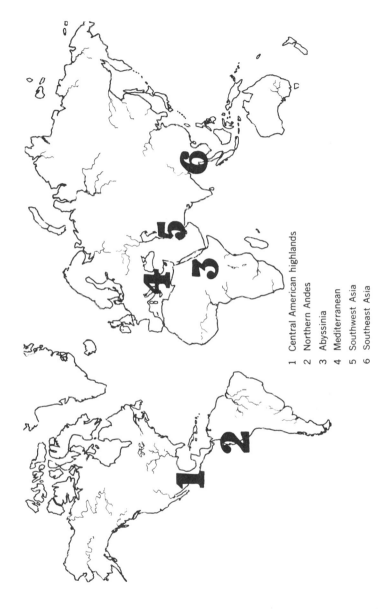

1 Central American highlands
2 Northern Andes
3 Abyssinia
4 Mediterranean
5 Southwest Asia
6 Southeast Asia

Figure 2-5.   Vavilov's centers of plant domestication.

the center of origin of an economic plant species is likely to be near the area in which the largest number of varieties of that species grow. Plant-breeding work in Europe and North America with crop plants recruited from quite different parts of the world has tended to obscure this principle, but, as long as attention is confined to the materials utilized by less sophisticated, native peoples, the generalization holds up moderately well. The map in Fig. 2-5 shows the locations of six major centers of plant domestication established by Vavilov as a result of his studies.

A more recent attempt to analyze the geography of plant domestication has been made by Jack R. Harlan in his book *Crops and Man,* published in 1975. Harlan finds the picture to be less obviously one of "centers" (although he locates three of these — the Near East, North China, and Mesoamerica); rather he associates large areas of plant domestication (he calls them "non-centers") with these centers. Thus, there is an African non-center, a southeast Asian non-center, and a South American non-center. Harlan envisages "some stimulation and feedback in terms of ideas, techniques, or materials between center and non-center within each system" (1975, p. 53).

Expeditions

A knowledge of the areas of origin of economic plants is important when attempts are made to collect closely related wild material from which desirable characteristics of disease resistance, climatic adaptation, and so on, may be incorporated into the crop plant in a program of breeding. Thus, in this century several countries have sent expeditions to the source of the potato (*Solanum tuberosum*) in the northern Andes of South America, to collect wild and cultivated potatoes, which have then been grown in selected gardens in the various countries. Many other examples could be cited (e.g., safflower, *Carthamus tinctorius,* Chapter 8).

Not only may expeditions provide for the improvement of crop plants in areas already under cultivation, but their findings may also enable agriculture to be carried to new areas for which there is currently no variety or race suitable for cultivation. This can be illustrated by the success that has attended Australian efforts to increase the carrying capacity of natural grasslands on that continent by collecting and introducing appropriate plants. Grasses (e.g., *Phalaris tuberosa*) and a clover (*Trifolium subterraneum*) form the basis of improvements in their temperate grazing lands. Although these most important species first came to Australia from Europe more or less accidentally, the Australian government has since then sent several expeditions to the more arid parts of the Mediterranean region to collect more productive and ecologically tolerant races of these and other species. They have sent other expeditions to Africa for grasses and to the American tropics for leguminous forage plants to stock tropical pastures in northern Australia. Similar efforts may be expected from nations whose agricultural development is beginning or expanding.

3

Plants as Stimuli of
Exploration and Exploitation

Spices

In tropical communities, the diet has always contained monotonous staples such as starchy grains or "roots." Consequently, it is not surprising that in tropical countries the use of spices became very important at an early stage in history.

Spices are edible materials that are not consumed so much for their food value as for their aromatic, flavor-producing qualities (Fig. 3-1). There is no sharp line of distinction between "spices," which are usually of tropical origin, and the largely temperate "herbs," which also have culinary use. The flavor and aroma are due to essential oils—organic substances of varied composition which generally tend to have relatively small molecules, making them volatile. The essential oils often either belong to the chemical group of hydrocarbons called *terpenes* or are derivatives from them. The oils may be extracted from plant tissues by organic solvents that are then distilled off to leave the "oil" itself (Fig. 3-2).

The function of spices in the diet is threefold. First, they save the diet from becoming monotonous. Second, they disguise the unpleasant flavor of meat that is not fresh—an important matter in tropical regions before the advent of refrigeration. Third, they increase the rate of perspiration and therefore cause

Figure 3-1. A collection of spices. Clockwise from the top lefthand corner: cinnamon "quills"; a portion of a leafy shoot of vanilla (*Vanilla planifolia*), and a dried "bean" from this orchid; a dried "hand" (the branched rhizome) of ginger; two dried portions of turmeric rhizome; cloves; and (center) capsicum peppers.

cooling of the body—another important consideration in tropical regions. In addition to these three genuine qualities, there are several other allegedly valuable properties of spices. For example, it has been claimed that they aid the digestive processes. They have also been assumed to act as preservatives and have been used as "deodorants," possibly because they can cover a strong, unpleasant odor with an even stronger but pleasant one.

Spices have sometimes been so important that they have been used in place of money. In medieval England, rents and taxes were often exacted in "peppercorns," the dried berries of the true pepper plant. Much of the exploration of

Figure 3-2. An herb garden in which essential oils are being extracted from some of the plants. Similar essential oils give spices their aromas. From H. Brunschwig, *Liber de Arte Distillandi de Simplicibus*, 1500.

the world during the fifteenth and sixteenth centuries was incidental to the quest for spices. The rediscovery of the American continent by Columbus was directly inspired by the search for a shorter route to the spices of the Indies, particularly pepper (Fig. 3-3), and the cost of Magellan's ill-fated voyage around the world (1519–1522) was completely paid for by the cloves and other spices that the one surviving ship brought back to Europe.

The use and cultivation of spice plants goes back to the beginning of history, and in China, as well as in the ancient civilizations of Egypt, Greece, and Rome, spices were highly prized. One famous spice, cinnamon, is mentioned in the Song of Solomon and the Book of Proverbs. It had already been used in anointing and embalming the dead in ancient Egypt.

Arabs supplied spices to the Egyptians, Greeks, and Romans, but they jealously concealed the sources of cinnamon and other spices as well as their manner of obtaining them. Cinnamon was so rare that in A.D. 65, a year's supply to Rome was used up in the burial ceremonies of Poppaea, the wife of the Emperor Nero. In fact, cinnamon came from Sri Lanka (formerly known as Ceylon), whence it was brought to the west coast of India, where the Arab traders bought it. The Arabs themselves conveyed it by a land route to Arabia, and from there to Egypt and Europe. Marco Polo's 24-year journey, which began in 1271 from Venice and took him through the Far East, helped to expose the origin of the Arabs' supply of spices but, strangely, he did not mention seeing cinnamon in Sri Lanka.

Old World Spices

Many spices are products of the islands of Asia rather than the land mass, and in this connection one of the most famous groups of islands is the Moluccas, the so-called "Spice Islands," to which nutmeg and clove trees were restricted as wild plants. Next in importance is Sri Lanka, which to this day is almost the only supplier of true cinnamon, produced from the bark of the evergreen shrub *Cinnamomum zeylanicum,* a member of the Lauraceae—the laurel family.

Cinnamon plants, which may be grown on plantations under semiwild conditions, are cut back to the roots. The new shoots, which develop as long, straight branches, are allowed to grow for two years. Then the shrub is again cut back to the roots. Two longitudinal slits are made in the long shoots that have been severed, and the bark is peeled off in three-foot lengths, each equivalent to half the bark of the branch. These lengths of bark are allowed to lie for a day and partly ferment. Then the outer cork is scraped off and the remainder of the bark is dried and broken into more convenient lengths to produce the so-called cinnamon "quills." These quills may be pulverized later to produce the ground spice with which we are most familiar.

Much of the cinnamon consumed in the United States today comes from a different species, *Cinnamomum cassia,* the so-called "cassia" of China, Indochina, and Indonesia. It has a stronger flavor than the true cinnamon.

Cinnamon is just one of the Asiatic spices, the search for which, in the fifteenth century, stimulated the wonderful voyages of Portuguese sailors in their "caravels." These were begun under the influence of Prince Henry "the Navigator." In 1416, Prince Henry founded a school of navigation at Sagres, near Cape St. Vincent, in Portugal, and thereafter devoted himself to planning and equipping voyages of exploration until his death in 1460. The voyages continued, and cinnamon was the prize for Vasco da Gama, who sailed in 1497 from Portugal around the Cape of Good Hope to east Africa and thence across the Indian Ocean to the Malabar coast.

Earlier, in 1470, the Portuguese had reached the Guinea coast of Africa, and they proceeded to exploit it. They named four areas after their principal products. Translated into English these names are: the Grain Coast (which is now roughly the area covered by Liberia), the Ivory Coast, the Gold Coast (which has become Ghana and Togo), and the Slave Coast (now Dahomey and Nigeria).

The Grain Coast requires explanation. The product of this coast was not cereal grains but "grains of paradise" — the seeds of a small ginger-like plant, *Aframomum melegueta*, which belongs to the ginger family, the Zingiberaceae. These seeds are very pungent and were relished for having a better flavor than the true peppers, which are the berries of the vine *Piper nigrum* (Fig. 3-3).

Figure 3-3. Stylized representation of true pepper (*Piper nigrum*). From Jacques d'Alechamps, *Historia Generalis Plantarum*, Vol. II, 1587.

Plants as Stimuli of Exploration and Exploitation

The grains of paradise were eventually displaced in public esteem by capsicum peppers from the New World, because the latter could be produced in much greater quantity than the relatively rare grains of paradise. Today, capsicum peppers (Fig. 3-4), the fruits of *Capsicum* spp. (Solanaceae), are particularly used to flavor stews, curries, and chilies.

Figure 3-4. A capsicum pepper plant (*Capsicum annuum*) showing one shape and size that the fruits (in this case, bright red) may assume. Grown at University of California Botanical Garden.

Curry powder contains, among other spices, ground, dried capsicum peppers, and also turmeric from the rhizomes or underground stems of *Curcuma longa* (another member of the Zingiberaceae). Turmeric helps to color the curry powder, for it has long been used as a dye plant as well as a spice. Curry powder may also contain ginger, derived from the rhizome of *Zingiber officinale* (Fig. 3-5), as well as fenugreek, the spice derived from the ground seeds of *Trigonella foenum-graecum* of the Leguminosae, and ground oregano and cumin from the leaves of *Origanum vulgare* (Labiatae) and *Cuminum cyminum* (Umbelliferae), respectively. Garlic, from the bulbs of *Allium sativum* (Amaryllidaceae), is also a constituent.

Following their circumnavigation of Africa in 1497, the Portuguese took control of much of the Indian Ocean and extended their trading as far as China, where the port of Macao still survives as a Portuguese enclave. Goa, in India, remained a Portuguese possession until recently. The Portuguese occupied

Sri Lanka with the particular intention of controlling cinnamon production, and they held a virtual monopoly of the Indian Ocean spice trade for well over a century. Later, the Dutch appropriated their monopoly.

Dutch control of the spices of the East Indies was the eventual outcome of expeditions begun by van Houtman, who returned to Holland in 1597 from his first trip with three shiploads of pepper and nutmeg. Fighting off Portuguese and British competition, the Dutch established the headquarters of their East India Company at Batavia, in Java. In 1621 they issued an order for the destruction of all clove and nutmeg trees on each of the Molucca islands except Amboyna and Ternate and the Banda islands. By cutting the production of

Figure 3-5. Plant of ginger (*Zingiber officinale*) showing the rhizome from which the dried ginger "hands" are made. Grown at University of California Botanical Garden.

these spices to only a quarter of the previous level, they forced the prices in Europe up to the very maximum.

Dutch control of Sri Lanka was established in 1656, and their monopoly of cinnamon production lasted until 1833. Actually, the deliberate cultivation of cinnamon bushes did not begin until 1770; prior to this time, wild plants were used as the source of the spice. Vast fortunes were made in this exploitative manner by the shareholders of the Dutch East India Company, yet these fortunes, it should be remembered, produced patronage of the arts at home in Holland.

The nutmeg tree, *Myristica fragrans,* belongs to a small family, the Myristicaceae. Not all nutmeg trees are capable of producing nutmegs, for this is a dioecious species. Some trees produce only staminate flowers, but the others that produce only pistillate flowers are the sources of the fruits and seeds. The fruits (Fig. 3-6) look rather like large apricots, and inside the orange-yellow pulp is a large, hard, brown seed, the nutmeg itself. It may be ground and used like cinnamon.

Figure 3-6. (Clockwise from top left) Nutmeg fruit; mace; nutmeg; and fruit cut open to show nutmeg and mace in place. Photograph by W. H. Hodge from Ward's Natural Science Establishment, Inc. Reproduced by permission.

The nutmeg is surrounded by a thin, brittle shell (the seed coat), surrounded in turn by an additional, red-colored, reticulate, fleshy layer. This is the mace, which is technically an aril, an extra covering over the seed within the fruit. Mace itself serves as a distinct spice, containing quite different essential oils from those of the nutmeg seed; it provides a delicate flavoring for sauces, ketchups, and savory dishes.

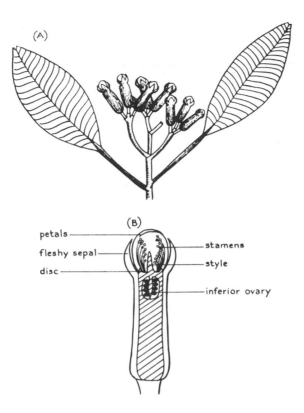

(A)

(B)

petals ————
fleshy sepal ———
disc ————

——— stamens
——— style
———— inferior ovary

Figure 3-7. (A) Diagram of inflorescence of clove tree (*Eugenia aromatica*) showing flower buds (cloves). (B) Diagrammatic longitudinal section through a flower bud. From L. S. Cobley, *An Introduction to the Botany of Tropical Crops.* London: Longmans, Green & Co., 1956. Reproduced by permission.

Although native to the Moluccas, most nutmeg trees today are grown in the West Indies (where, in 1955, Hurricane Janet destroyed 40% of the world crop by flattening plantations on the island of Grenada).

Cloves are quite different from the previously mentioned spices. Their name comes from the French word for nail, *un clou*, and this is an apt description of the appearance of the clove itself (Fig. 3-7). Cloves are dried, unopened flower buds of *Eugenia aromatica*, a small evergreen tree of the Myrtaceae. A clove tree is a wonderful sight when it is covered with red blossoms, but, since the flower buds are collected and dried, few trees reach this stage.

Cloves are known to have been used in China in the third century B.C., where, apart from other uses, they were ordered to be used as breath-sweeteners by courtiers addressing the emperor. They were also known by the Romans. They were introduced into the rest of Europe during the Middle Ages. In all cases they came from the Moluccas. At present they are used to flavor pies, candy, mouth washes and dentifrices; clove oil, the essential oil extracted from them, has been used for the relief of toothache, and is used in biology as a histological clearing agent. Clove oil also has more recent utility, as a source from which chemists may make synthetic vanillin, yet another spice substance.

In the seventeenth and eighteenth centuries, the trade in nutmeg and cloves was a Dutch monopoly. Eventually, however, smugglers, at great risk, got spices out of the Dutch possessions and spread them to other parts of the world. Assisting in this process was the replacement of Dutch rule in many areas in the Indian Ocean by British administration, and the replacement of the Dutch East India Company as a trading power by its British equivalent. Thus, nutmeg became established in Penang, in Malaya, and particularly in Grenada, in the British West Indies. Cloves were successfully grown by the French in Mauritius and Réunion in 1770; they were carried from there to the British East African colony of Zanzibar and the neighboring island of Pemba, where the vast majority of the present-day clove plantations are located in what is now Tanzania.

In 1672, Elihu Yale entered the spice trade in India (first as a clerk for the British East India Company). From the fortune which he amassed came the foundation of Yale University.

New World Spices

We have already seen that it was the discovery of the New World that added capsicum peppers to the spice trade. Capsicum peppers vary all the way from big, green bell peppers, which are not peppery at all, to small, red chili peppers. Nowadays, some of the hottest of these come from Africa, even though this is a spice plant native to the New World. Actually, there are only about four closely related species of *Capsicum* (Solanaceae) involved in the production of economically useful peppers, and bell peppers and chili peppers may both be produced by the same species, *Capsicum annuum* and *C. frutescens*. Capsicum peppers are rich in vitamin C, and also have laxative properties.

The pungent principle in capsicum peppers is a volatile phenolic compound called capsaicin ($C_{18}H_{23}NO_3$), a substance so powerfully affecting human taste buds that even a dilution of 1:1,000,000 of water is detectable. Its presence or absence in a pepper plant is due to variation in a single gene. When it is present, the greatest concentration of capsaicin is found in the placenta, the tissue joining the seeds to the fruit.

Capsicum peppers are known from prehistoric burial sites in Peru, and they were widely cultivated in the New World before the arrival of Columbus. However, the New World has not contributed nearly so many spices as it has received from Asia.

There is one major spice derived from tropical America that is unusual in several ways. This is vanilla, which is obtained from an orchid, *Vanilla planifolia*, normally growing as a climber on trees. Its flavoring material, vanillin, is quite gentle to the taste and is, of course, much used in the flavoring of milk puddings, chocolate, and ice cream. Strangely enough, it is a fairly close chemical relative of the hot capsaicin from the capsicum peppers. Vanilla is obtained from the pods of the vanilla plant; these pods are collected and then allowed to dry slowly, fermenting at the same time. The characteristic flavor and odor, which are absent from the unfermented bean, gradually become apparent. Nowadays, vanillin is also obtained synthetically from clove oil.

It might be interesting to close this portion of the chapter by parading some of the spice plants that are still used today, illustrating how, in each one, a different plant part is used.

An example of a plant in which the roots are used to provide an essential oil is the horseradish, *Armoracia lapathifolia*, of the Cruciferae. This spice plant is unusual in a number of respects. It is temperate in origin, and appears to have been cultivated so long and propagated so extensively and continuously through the breaking off and replanting of portions of the root system that, whatever may have been its original power of reproducing by seed, this ability has been diminished. Even when horseradish is allowed to flower, it forms very few viable seeds.

As an example of the group of spices that are obtained from underground storage and reproductive stems called rhizomes, we may cite ginger, which is obtained from *Zingiber officinale*. Aerial stems give us cinnamon, from the bark of *Cinnamomum zeylanicum*. The leaves of a number of plants provide us with flavoring materials, perhaps the best known of which is bay, obtained from the leaves of the tree *Laurus nobilis* of the Lauraceae. Flower buds provide us with cloves, while fruits may be exemplified by the capsicum peppers and the true peppers. Seeds are represented by fenugreek.

Most remarkable, perhaps, is the use of the stigmas of the saffron, *Crocus sativus* (Iridaceae), which provide the most expensive spice of all. Seventy thousand flowers are needed to provide a pound of the spice. Fortunately, just a pinch of saffron in hot water gives an intriguing taste and a rich golden color to rice and baked goods. Much saffron was grown in England in the Middle Ages to provide the material for saffron cakes. It is also an essential ingredient in the making of *arroz con pollo*, the famous rice-chicken dish of the Spanish world.

Timber

The search for spices and shorter routes for bringing them to Europe constituted a powerful stimulus for exploration and exploitation of newly discovered territories, and naval power became necessary for the protection of the trade routes from pirates. And there were botanical problems even in the construction and fitting-out of naval ships.

From the beginning of the seventeenth century to the middle of the nineteenth, vast quantities of timber were used in the construction of ships. Not until the famous battle in Hampton Roads in 1862, when the ironclad *Virginia*, originally the *Merrimac*, defeated the wooden *Congress* and *Cumberland* and drew with the *Monitor*, was the fate of wooden ships sealed.

During the era of the wooden ships, the problems faced by the British Navy were characteristic. The hulls of their ships were made of oakwood, utilizing timbers of a curved form produced by trees growing in the open rather than in forests. Unfortunately, however, oak trees are slow in growing, taking roughly a century to reach adequate size. Until about 1650, British naval demands for oak timber were easily met from the oak woodlands of southern England; but then, as these sources became exhausted, oak had to be imported from Germany, the American colonies, and elsewhere. The demand became so great that "green," unseasoned timber had to be used, and the hulls of ships rotted at a fantastic rate. The hull of H.M.S. *Queen Charlotte*, for example, which was launched in 1810, was completely rotted before she ever put to sea. Such rotting was due largely to attack by fungi, particularly at the waterline.

The construction of masts and spars also presented difficulties. These ship's parts were made of softwoods derived from coniferous trees, whose growth in forest conditions was necessary to produce tall, unbranched trunks. However, there have never been any such forests in the British Isles, and the spars had to be obtained from Scandinavian coniferous forests. Consequently, access to Baltic timber ports was a necessity for the British fleets, and the British were continuously engaged in naval operations in and around the Baltic Sea—a circumstance that adjacent countries found objectionable. As a result, after about 1652 the British Navy began to use for masts timber that had been imported from northeastern North America.

Nevertheless, during the Dutch Wars (1652–1674), the American Revolution, and the Napoleonic Wars (at the beginning of the nineteenth century), British naval strength was severely diminished through shortages of appropriate timber. Especially during the war with Napoleon, it was only by retaining their sources of timber in Canada that the British were able to achieve naval victories.

A partial solution to the shortage of oak for shipbuilding was found in the use of tropical hardwoods, notably teak, from the southeast Asian tree *Tectona grandis*. This easily worked and extraordinarily durable wood contains a resinous oil that protects it from attack by fungi and animals, and prevents rusting of iron nails. Along with spices, cotton, and other consumer goods, teak was yet another reason for the growth and consolidation of the British Empire.

The Potato Famine and Irish Emigration

Not only have plants stimulated exploration and exploitation, they have also been responsible — often in a negative way — for human migrations. The failure of the potato (Fig. 3-8) to support the Irish people in the middle of the nineteenth century produced one of the most dreadful famines in the history of the Western world, followed by an unparalleled migration.

Figure 3-8. Potato plant (*Solanum tuberosum*). From Gaspard Bauhin, *Prodromus Theatri Botanici*, 1620.

The potato, *Solanum tuberosum*, was introduced into Ireland at the end of the sixteenth century and was so rapidly adopted by the poverty-stricken population that within fifty years it was the staple food of the whole country. It is an excellent starch source, and it has been estimated that seven pounds of potatoes will satisfy a man's daily requirements in calories (3,000), protein, and iron, as well as vitamins B and C. Half the phosphorus and one-tenth of the calcium requirements will also be supplied, and the remainder of man's dietary requirements can be satisfied by a pint of milk.

On this diet the Irish peasantry survived until, in 1845 and 1846, the "potato blight," a fungus disease caused by *Phytophthora infestans*, swept over Europe, blackening the leaves of the plants and causing their tubers to rot. Purely vegetative propagation of this plant, done by planting portions of the potato tuber that bear "eyes" (shoot buds), had led to uniformity of genetical constitution of the plants in any area. Technically speaking, all the plants "belonged to the same clone." This meant that once the disease entered a country, all the plants were equally susceptible to it and the epidemic was unstoppable. In Ireland, over a million persons died of famine and disease, and another million were forced to emigrate within the next few years, mostly to the New World. As the potato's chief biographer, Redcliffe Salaman, has written, "History has few parallels to such a disaster—a disaster due to the criminal folly of allowing a single, cheaply produced foodstuff to dominate the dietary of the people." While it might seem that we should have learned our lesson from this, we will see in Chapter 9 that in some tropical countries the developing social structures rest almost entirely on the income from a single export crop, which could be wiped out by disease.

4

Possible Pre-Columbian Contacts
between the Old and New Worlds

The famous Swiss botanist Alphonse de Candolle concluded that in the the history of crop plants there is no evidence of communications between the peoples of the Old and New Worlds before the discovery, or rediscovery, of America by Columbus. It is possible to hold this opinion almost unaltered today, although the subject has provoked heated discussions between some who believe that there were prehistoric contacts between the Americas and Africa, Asia, and Europe, and those who would deny that such links could have occurred. We know that Norsemen reached eastern North America about 1000 A.D., possibly even preceded by Irish monks, and it is possible that there were rare contacts in the south; but as far as the movement of economic plants is concerned, these voyages do not seem to have been of major importance.

It is almost certain that when human beings entered North America from Eastern Asia—probably on foot and accompanied by dogs—they did so through the region that is now the Bering Straits. Most likely, this migration came during or immediately after the last glaciation of the Ice Age; at any rate, it occurred between 15,000 and 100,000 years ago. From this entry, human beings spread gradually over the continent.

People were probably never more than gatherers and hunters during this migration, however, and we must presume that agriculture in the New World either evolved separately from its evolution in the Old World, or else was brought there later from the Old World. All the convincing evidence indicates that the New World inhabitants developed agriculture unaided up to the state in which the Spanish explorers found it, with its emphasis on maize, beans, and squashes. After the Spanish discovery, European touches were added to the indigenous New World agriculture, while many New World plants, such as cassava, maize, and peanuts, were exported to other tropical and subtropical regions. The most important single fact is that the typical food plants of the New World are almost all strikingly different from those of the Old World, not only taxonomically but also in their very natures.

In the New World, the characteristic pre-Columbian cereal was maize; in the Old World, depending on the region and the climate, it was rice, sorghum, or millets in tropical regions, and wheat, rye, barley, or oats in temperate regions. The characteristic legumes of the New World consisted of several beans of the genus *Phaseolus*; indeed, the area was particularly rich in beans of agricultural significance. In addition, peanuts (*Arachis hypogaea*) are also native to the Western Hemisphere. Some of the amino acids present in the proteins of the beans are especially significant because they complement those in maize corn grain to provide a full and balanced human diet (see Chapter 8). In the Old World, there was a poorer selection of leguminous plants; and, except for a few tropical beans and soybeans (*Glycine max*) in China the most significant legumes were peas (*Pisum sativum*), lentils (*Lens esculenta*), and broad beans (*Vicia faba*).

Squashes were important in the New World; many species of the genus *Cucurbita* (Cucurbitaceae) played an important role in the diet of New World Indians, and the genus is unknown wild outside the Americas. The commonly cultivated species of this genus are not found growing wild and are known only from their association with man—a tribute to their ancient domestication or derivation. They are known to have formed a part of the diet of Peruvian and Mexican Indians at least as far back as 3000 B.C. On the other hand, *Cucurbitaceae* were relatively unimportant in the Old World, and, except for watermelons and cucumbers, there are few contributions from this family.

Among "root" crops, cassava (*Manihot esculenta*) and tania (*Xanthosoma sagittifolium*) are characteristically New World products, whereas, in the Old World, different species of yam (*Dioscorea* spp.) and the taro or dasheen (*Colocasia esculenta*) were the most frequently cultivated. To spice their foods, New World Indians used capsicum peppers, whereas in the Old World the true pepper (*Piper nigrum*) and also grains of paradise (*Aframomum melegueta*) were used.

Even when the same plant genus was used in both hemispheres, characteristically different species were involved, usually in rather different fashions. Thus, in the genus *Solanum*, *S. tuberosum* (the "Irish" potato) is native to South America; the underground stem tuber was put to use by indigenous people. In the Old World, the species of *Solanum* most frequently encountered in the diet of tropical African and Asian peoples was *Solanum melongena*, the aubergine or eggplant, in which the fruit was cooked as a vegetable.

These lists are so strikingly different for the two continents that there would seem no room for any other thought but that agriculture evolved separately in each continent. Yet some people are unwilling to believe that man could develop to a high level of efficiency the deliberate growing of plants for food, clothing, and ornament independently in two areas of the world. They postulate cultural contacts between the Old World and the New World, after the origin of agriculture but before 1492. Thus there has been a great deal of controversy between the "diffusionists," who believe in this diffusion of agriculture, and the "inventionists," who believe that man has been capable of evolving the agricultural idea more than once. Therefore, it is important to consider other evidence that New World agriculture differs in character as well as materials from that of the western part of the Old World.

None of the principal New World agricultural plants was particularly suited for such bulk treatment as sowing broadcast, reaping, and threshing; on the other hand, this handling of masses of plants rather than individuals is characteristic of the cereal-growing of the Old World, whether one thinks of tropical rice or temperate wheat and barley. New World farmers north of Panama lacked domestic animals for plowing, carrying, and producing milk, manure, wool, and meat. Yet all of these were features of Old World agriculture since prehistoric times. In South America these tasks could have been performed by llamas, vicunas, and similar animals of the camel tribe, but there is little evidence that they were put to such uses as a regular feature of the agricultural system.

If New World civilizations really had contacts with the Old World, it is astonishing that they failed to incorporate the wheel in their way of life — particularly the dwellers in drier regions, where the wheel would have been most useful. The existence of wheeled toys from Mexico shows that the *principle* was understood, but the agricultural utility of wheels seems not to have been appreciated.

What then are the botanical bases for belief that there were cultural connections in pre-Columbian days? Some years ago anthropologist Carleton Coon suggested that the controversy actually boils down to the interpretation of the history of a small number of plants. We should consider the coconut, *Cocos nucifera*; the calabash or gourd, *Lagenaria siceraria*; the sweet potato, *Ipomoea batatas*; the peanut, *Arachis hypogaea*; maize, *Zea mays*; and the cotton genus, *Gossypium*. For each of the first five, some evidence, of varying reliability, has been produced to show that these species existed in both the New and Old Worlds before or very soon after the Columbian discovery. In the case of cotton, there is no evidence that any one extant species of the genus was common to the New and Old Worlds prior to 1492, even though cotton was used for spinning and weaving in both. There is, however, evidence that the cultivated cottons of the New World contain genetic material found in Old World species in combination with genetic material of New World origin.

We shall discuss these six kinds of plants here, although maize will be dealt with in more detail later.

The Coconut

The coconut palm, which is widespread in the tropics between 20 and 25 degrees latitude north and south of the equator, generally needs a humid climate for its best development, although it can be seen growing in areas with a rainfall as low as 25 inches per year. It appears to need a sandy soil, and, perhaps for this reason as much as any other, it is largely confined to coastal situations. Perhaps the most typical sight of the tropics is a sandy beach backed by gracefully curved coconut palms (Fig. 4-1).

The coconut palm is a multi-purpose plant of extreme value to tropical people. The "milk" from the seed (actually a liquid endosperm—Fig. 4-2) is free from bacteria and other organisms that may cause disease, and, therefore,

Figure 4-1. Coconut palms (*Cocos nucifera*) growing on a coastal sandbar near Negombo, Sri Lanka.

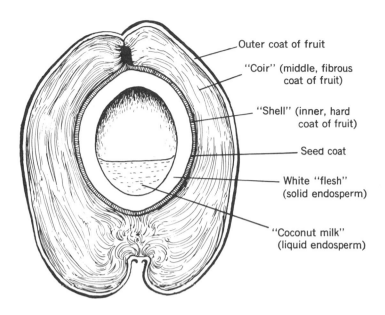

Figure 4-2. Diagrammatic cross section of a coconut fruit.

has great value in areas where natural water supplies may be contaminated. The solid portion of the endosperm may be eaten directly or dried to produce copra (from which coconut oil may be extracted later). The husks of the fruit are useful as containers, and the fiber (the coir), which is the middle layer of the fruit wall, is made into rope and matting. The leaves from the tree are used in thatching cottages. Sap from the stem may be tapped by cutting the large sheathing leaf surrounding the opening flowers, and, when evaporated, provides a sugar or, when fermented, an alcoholic drink.

With a plant as valuable as this, it is not surprising that man has taken a great part in dispersing the coconut palm throughout the tropics of the world — so much so, in fact, that there is considerable doubt as to the true geographical area of its origin. One of the first serious attempts to localize its origin was made by O. F. Cook, who concluded that the species is native to the New World and was dispersed from there. Indeed, there is historical evidence that the coconut palm was growing in the Isthmus of Panama when the Spaniards first arrived. However, if this was the case, it was growing only on the Pacific side as far north as Costa Rica, and southward along the coast to Colombia. It was missing from the Atlantic Coast, suggesting to some botanists that the coconut palm may have arrived in the New World relatively shortly before the Spanish discovery. This is backed by the accounts of early Spanish explorers who reported that the natives had few uses for the palm and that at least some believed it had arrived recently from overseas.

Those who believe that the coconut palm is native to the New World have pointed out that the 20 other species that have been placed in the genus *Cocos* are all restricted to the New World. However, recent taxonomic revisions of the palm family suggest that this is irrelevant to the question of the origin of the coconut palm itself, for it is now recognized that these other species are only distantly related to *Cocos nucifera*. In fact, it has been proposed that they should be separated into other genera, leaving the coconut palm as the only representative of the genus *Cocos*. The coconut palm may actually be more closely related to palms of the Indian Ocean, even those of eastern Africa, than it is to the New World's native palm species. As a result, the more generally accepted view, first put forward by Beccari, an Italian palm specialist, is that it originated in southeast Asia. There are even fossil records from India, New Zealand, and the Marianas. Marco Polo saw coconut palms in Asia and there are other accounts of them dating back to the ninth century. The Sanskrit word for the dried endosperm is *khorpara,* which has become *copra* in modern times. All of these kinds of evidence, assembled by geographer Jonathan Sauer, in the de Candolle tradition, indicate the Old World origin of *Cocos nucifera*.

An interesting piece of indirect evidence on the naturalness of the occurrence of the coconut palm on the Indian and Pacific Ocean islands is provided by the dependence upon it of a large crab (*Birgus latro*) which lives in burrows in the sand and lines them with fibers from the husks of the coconuts. At night the crabs feed upon fallen coconuts (which they hammer open with their claws) or will even climb the palms and pluck them. It is inconceivable that such a high degree of specialization could be reached quickly and, as a consequence, the distribution of the crab gives a minimal estimate of the range of the coconut palm before man began to move it around. The crab is found in the Indian Ocean and on Madagascar as well as on a number of Pacific Ocean islands (not including Hawaii). It does not occur on the coast of Central America.

There is no doubt that, in addition, the coconut has been deliberately transported from place to place by man. It may have been carried from Asia to West Africa by Portuguese mariners returning to Europe around the Cape of Good Hope. These same voyagers probably also introduced it to the east coast of South America. Actually, Spaniards saw coconuts brought by Portuguese from Asia before they discovered them for themselves in the New World and, consequently, used the Portuguese name "cocos" for them.

However, even if the coconut palm was present on both sides of the Pacific Ocean in pre-Columbian days, this does not mean that the fruits were carried across the ocean by man, for they are excellently adapted for distribution by natural means, using sea currents. Because of the air trapped between the coir fibers in the fruit wall, coconut fruits float easily and sea water never comes in contact with the seed. Consequently, germination is possible after the fruit is washed up on the shore, provided that it arrives in a suitable sandy habitat and survives attack by wild hogs, rodents, and crabs.

Thus, although the trans-Pacific journey from southeastern Asia to the western side of the Isthmus of Panama might possibly have been the result of human carriage, it could also have been the result of natural flotation. All around the world the sandy beaches of the tropics bear a remarkably uniform flora. Many of the species of shore plants are the same in the Old World and in the New, but these are naturally distributed species and, because they have no value to man, no one has suggested that they indicate cultural contacts across the oceans. In all probability we should not attach any great significance to the presence of the coconut in both hemispheres.

The Calabash or Gourd

The calabash or gourd probably falls into the same category as the coconut. This plant is *Lagenaria siceraria* (Fig. 4-3), a common tropical member of the Cucurbitaceae. Although the flesh of the hard-walled fruits of this species is edible, it is rarely consumed by man because it is bitter to the taste. More often, the fruits are dried and cut open, and the flesh and seeds are scooped out. The fruit can then be used to store and carry solids and liquids, and the seeds, if needed for food, can be roasted. There is excellent evidence that, in prehistoric times, the fruits of the calabash were being used as containers both in the Old World and the New.

Figure 4-3. The calabash gourd plant (*Lagenaria siceraria*) with fruit. From Rumphius (G. E. Rumph), *Herbarium Amboinense*, 1747.

Specimens have been found in an Egyptian tomb dated about 2500 B.C., in Peruvian burials dated at about 2700 B.C., in Mexican caves from about 7000 B.C. onwards, and in a cave in Thailand from about 7000 B.C. In Peru, the fruits, or at least the seeds, were eaten also. The calabash does not occur as a wild plant today, except in a few places in Africa, and it seems most likely that it had its origin in that continent. This is substantiated by the presence of three other species of *Lagenaria* in Africa.

Experiments by T. W. Whitaker and G. F. Carter in which calabash gourds were placed in sea water show that the gourds can float for as long as two years without the seeds inside losing their capacity to germinate. Thus, the gourds would have had plenty of time to drift across the Atlantic Ocean. Only 1400 miles separate the coasts of Sierra Leone and Brazil, although the ocean is wider in southern areas where the South Equatorial Current can pick up fruits and carry them across. Experiments have shown that corked bottles can be transported across the ocean in several months.

Even a single plant will do to start a population of the calabash, because both pistillate and staminate flowers are found on the same plant, which is self-fertile. Thus, if the gourd, after being transported, is thrown high onto the beach by a storm and is fractured so that the seeds escape (or if the gourd should be picked up and carried into a village by curious beachcombers to be chopped open and then thrown out on the village trash heap), the seeds might germinate and establish the plant in the new situation.

These possibilities of natural distribution, then, place the calabash gourd in the same position as the coconut: the gourd may have been distributed naturally and still have been used by man on both sides of the Atlantic Ocean, particularly by people who did not find pottery making easy or congenial. Subsidiary uses of these gourds as floats for fishing nets would seem to be logical developments by people who had found them floating naturally in the sea. On the other hand, it seems unlikely that persons making transoceanic voyages would load their boats with such bulky but nearly inedible fruits. Consequently, the calabash probably cannot be used as an example of a species whose presence on both sides of the Atlantic Ocean speaks in favor of cultural contacts between the hemispheres in ancient times.

The Sweet Potato

The next species on our list is the sweet potato, *Ipomoea batatas*, of the Convolvulaceae (Fig. 4-4). Here, again, there is good evidence that the plant was present in both New and Old Worlds prior to 1492. The economically important part of this plant is the swollen root tuber, which is a valuable starch source for tropical peoples, and, in addition, is rich in sugar (while the yellow color in the roots is due to carotene, which is a precursor of vitamin A). The roots also serve as a good source of iron and calcium. The sweet potato is always propagated vegetatively, usually by planting stem cuttings or portions of tubers. Flowering is not common, and seed is produced even more rarely, a fate one might expect for a crop plant that has been continuously propagated by vegetative means.

Figure 4-4.   Sweet potato plant (*Ipomoea batatas*) bearing tubers derived from adventitious roots. From W. Piso and G. Marcgrave, *Historiae Naturalis Brasiliae*, 1648.

The sweet potato is generally assumed to have originated in the American continent; recent studies point to tuberless climbing plants collected in tropical Central and South America, as representing either its progenitor or as descendants from a common ancestor. Nevertheless, it was early recognized in the islands of the South Pacific. When the Polynesian islands were visited by Europeans in the eighteenth century, sweet potatoes were found to be in general use by their inhabitants. Thus, the sweet potato was in Easter Island when that island was discovered by Roggeveen in 1722, and it was in the Hawaiian Islands at the time of their discovery by Captain Cook in 1778. Cook also found it in New Zealand in 1769. However, it has been objected that these records do not prove that the sweet potato was present in the Old World before 1492 because the first European voyagers in the Pacific Ocean were not British, French, or Dutch, but Spanish and Portuguese.

Donald Brand, of the University of Texas, who has looked carefully at the older literature, believes that Portuguese voyagers carried the sweet potato from eastern South America to western India before 1505. From there, it was carried by traders to Indonesia and picked up by Polynesians and others who carried it into the Pacific Ocean during the same century.

The sweet potato was least important in central Polynesia, where nearly all other food plants are of Southeast Asian origin, like the Polynesian people themselves. The sweet potato was important only on the eastern and southern sides of Polynesia where Southeast Asian plants were not so strongly established in favor. This suggests either that the sweet potato reached Polynesia from the American continent, or else that it arrived late and became established only where Asian plants did not predominate.

The sweet potato was probably transported by human beings, for it produces few fruits that could float across oceans; the germination of the seeds is irregular and the plants are self-sterile (which means that two plants must grow closely enough for cross-pollination to occur before further seed can be formed). Also, the tubers are susceptible to damage by seawater and thus could hardly survive a journey of their own undertaking.

One piece of evidence that the sweet potato was transported by man is that it appears to have carried its name with it throughout the Pacific. In the mountains of Peru, it is known by the name of *kumar*, and it is known by similar names throughout Polynesia. In Hawaii it is *uwala*; in New Zealand, the Maoris call it *kumara*. Obviously, a plant only carries its name around with it if it is distributed by man, and these names antedate history. Nevertheless, even this evidence has been questioned by those who point out that coastal Peruvians (who would more likely be concerned with the overseas transport of of the sweet potato) called it *apichu*, not *kumar*. (*Kumar* or *kumara*, in Polynesian, could be made up from *kuu*, meaning watery, and *mara*, meaning soft.)

Although the distribution of the sweet potato suggests a pre-Columbian contact between Polynesia and South America, and most students believe that this took place, it is likely that such contact represented an exceptional event rather than a common occurrence. There are two alternative theories regarding the means of contact: (1) either the Polynesians sailed to South America, where they picked up the sweet potato (possibly along with its name, given to them by captured prisoners), returning to plant it in Polynesia, or (2) South American Indians carried it to Polynesia, where they either became Polynesians or gave the sweet potato (and its name) to the Polynesians. Evidence can be produced to show that both alternatives are possible, and it should be remembered that they need not be likely, if we are not looking for continual intercourse between the areas.

First of all, let us take the possibility of Polynesian carriage. If Polynesians did voyage to South America, they would probably have done so before the fourteenth century. While they are known to have taken long voyages — for example, they colonized Hawaii from Tahiti (and radiocarbon dating shows that they may have arrived by the ninth or tenth century A.D.) — a journey to the South American continent would have been a tremendous voyage for them. Except by a very southern route, they would have had to face unfavorable trade winds. It is 2200 nautical miles even from Easter Island, the nearest known Polynesian settlement, to Peru. Yet the Polynesians did make long voyages elsewhere in the Pacific. On these journeys they used double canoes with matting sails, and they had many men to paddle (Fig. 4-5). The carefully shaped hulls were made from hollowed-out tree trunks, and were connected by a platform of lighter materials on which huts could be constructed.

Figure 4-5. Polynesian double canoe. From C. S. Coon, *The History of Man*. London: Jonathan Cape, 1955. Reproduced by permission.

There is no doubt that the Polynesians carried the sweet potato to Hawaii from some other part of Polynesia. In addition, they carried taro (*Colocasia esculenta*), and the candlenut tree (*Aleurites moluccana*), the oily fruits of which are used to make illuminating torches. They also transported the Ti plant (*Cordyline terminalis*), which is well known as the source material of "grass" skirts (made from its shredded leaves, which also serve as "plates" and food wrappers at feasts or luaus).

It may be supposed that if the Polynesians did reach South America, they engaged in battle with the South American Indians there, perhaps raiding villages from which they picked up the sweet potato along with captives who might have told them its name. The fact that they appear not to have picked up other plants of economic importance at this time could have been a result of the fleeting and hostile nature of their contact with the Indians. The Polynesians, however, have a rich heritage of legends, and strangely, there is none that records such an event in their history.

The second theory, the possibility that the Peruvian Indians carried the sweet potato to Polynesia, is also feasible. At the appropriate time in history there are known to have been advanced native cultures in Peru and, during this time, it

Figure 4-6.   Balsa raft used by Peruvian Indians. From a print by Benzoni, 1565.

is well known that the Peruvian Indians employed elaborate rafts (Fig. 4-6) of balsa wood for coastal cargo traffic. The balsa tree (*Ochroma lagopus*) produces the lightest and, therefore, the most buoyant wood in the world. With the aid of sails and paddles, the Peruvian balsa rafts are known to have been thoroughly navigable, and as long as the balsa wood could be water-proofed or was cut in a nonabsorptive state, there is no reason why these rafts could not journey as far as Polynesia.

Such a possibility had been proposed even before Thor Heyerdahl's epic recreation of it on the balsa raft Kon-Tiki in 1947. Bottles and even derelict ships had been seen to travel along such a route. What had not been demonstrated was, first, the ability of the balsa rafts to stay afloat long enough, and second, that an incentive existed for Peruvians to undertake such a voyage. Though Heyerdahl proved the ability of the rafts to make the journey, there is still no adequate reason put forward as to why the voyage should have been made and why, if it were made, only the sweet potato travelled by this route. We can, therefore, take our choice: either the Polynesians could have fetched the sweet potato or the Peruvian Indians could have taken it to Polynesia. Possibly both voyages were made.

In conclusion, if the sweet potato gives evidence of contacts between American Indians and members of the Old World human population before 1492, the evidence can hardly be said to be that of an important cultural contact, nor was the penetration of the Old World very deep. The problem, however, is worthy of exploration because it illustrates some of the difficulties that attend a reconstruction of the history of plants in relation to man.

Peanuts

Another interesting case is that of the peanut, *Arachis hypogaea*, a member of the Leguminosae. In this plant, the fruit is buried up to two inches under the soil by the elongation of the stem-like lower part of the flower, which previously bore the yellow flowers (Fig. 4-7). In some cases, fruits are actually produced from underground flowers. The fruits are elongated, oblong, indehiscent pods containing one to four seeds (the peanuts), depending on the variety (of which there are a great many). The wall of the fruit is constricted slightly between the seeds and is ridged. The seeds, in addition to containing starch reserves, contain globules of oil in their cells. This oil is much used nowadays in the manufacture of margarine as well as cooking and salad oils. Though South America is the home of the peanut, peanuts are now grown throughout the tropical world, with India the largest producer and China, West Africa, and the warmer southeastern states of the U.S. also important growing areas.

Although the peanut is known only from cultivation, related species of the genus *Arachis* are all native to South America, and peanut remains have been

Figure 4-7. Partially diagrammatic drawing of a portion of a peanut plant. Fruits are developing underground, having been buried by the elongation of the stem-like lower portion of each flower. From W. W. Robbins, *Botany of Crop Plants.* New York: McGraw-Hill Book Co., n.d. Reproduced by permission.

found in ancient Peruvian tombs dated at about 800 B.C. Yet the peanut is now so widely distributed in Africa and Asia that it must have arrived there a long time ago.

Was the distribution of the peanut to the Old World pre-Columbian? The Harvard botanist Oakes Ames observed that hump-backed peanuts that match the ancient Peruvian forms are grown today in south China, rather than in Peru, and later workers claimed that hump-backed peanuts reached China in pre-Columbian days. However, the center of *Arachis* differentiation is in Brazil and this alone should lead us to suspect that the world distribution of the peanut was taken on by the Portuguese. After Vasco da Gama's voyage around the Cape of Good Hope, the second Portuguese journey to India, in 1500, was from Lisbon to Brazil, and from there around the Cape of Good Hope to Goa, in India. In 1516, the Portuguese reached Canton, China, and later established their own colony of Macao, south of Hong Kong; it could be in this way that the hump-backed peanuts arrived in south China at an early date. Indeed, they have now also been found in Brazil, presumably the starting place of their saga.

Maize

Maize (discussed in more detail later) is pre-eminently the cereal of the New World. The oldest remains of maize known are many thousands of years old and are from Mexico. The oldest known ears are unusually small compared to those grown now and appear to have carried popcorn grain. Edgar Anderson, the famous American ethnobotanist, observed that small-eared varieties, also popcorns, are grown in the Naga Hills of Assam by tribes of head-hunters, and he suggested that this area of the Old World might be the source of maize. If true, maize was transported to the New World across the Pacific Ocean many thousands of years ago. There are also indications that maize was growing in China soon after Columbus discovered America; however, most authorities believe that the occurrence of these primitive forms of maize in Asia probably does not indicate a pre-Columbian existence there, although their introduction must have followed rapidly after the discovery of the New World by the Spanish and Portuguese.

How did these forms reach remote parts of Asia?

E. D. Merrill believes that the same voyages that carried the peanut also serve to explain the distribution of maize. The Portuguese trade route from Lisbon to Asia by way of Brazil and then around the Cape of Good Hope, was used for 165 years after its inception in 1500 (and it should be pointed out that popcorn, including a form like that which occurs in Assam today, is found in eastern Brazil). Maize may also have been brought to China by three quite different routes in the sixteenth and later centuries. The first of these would have been the Portuguese route already mentioned, from South America across the Atlantic and Indian Oceans. The second route would have involved Spanish carriage from Mexico to the Philippines and then to China. The third possible route would have been partly overland; that is, from the New World to Spain, across the Atlantic Ocean, then to the eastern Mediterranean, and from there to China overland along the Old Silk Trade Route, which Marco Polo had used long before.

As with all crop plants, we have to consider the possibility that maize may have been introduced in different ways at different times to the present parts of its distribution range. Thus, for West Africa, W. R. Stanton has shown that in the coastal forest areas Brazilian types of maize clearly brought across the Atlantic Ocean are predominant. On the other hand, in the northern savanna areas, the so-called "Arab" types, brought to the Mediterranean region and then carried across Africa by Arab traders, are in the majority.

Regardless of how maize was distributed, there is no convincing evidence that it was known anywhere outside the New World before the Columbian discovery.

Cotton

Our last concern in this connection is with cotton, and here it is with a complex of species that we must deal. There is no suggestion that any particular species of cotton now in cultivation in either the Eastern or Western Hemispheres was actually in cultivation in both hemispheres in pre-Columbian times; but there is, nevertheless, a problem concerning the genetic makeup of some of the species to be considered, and it has been suggested that man's influence was needed to produce the species of cotton that provide almost all of the present-day supply of cotton fiber.

All species of cotton belong to the genus *Gossypium* (in the family Malvaceae), and their seeds are borne inside fruits known as bolls (Figs. 4-8 and 4-9). From the seed coats, unicellular hairs grow out, which later lose their contents and become the familiar cotton fibers. Cotton fibers are of two sorts (Fig. 4-10), the long fibers known as lint and the short fibers known as fuzz. Each fiber consists of several cylindrical layers of cellulose, and collapses in a twisted fashion when dry. As a consequence, if the fiber is long enough it can be spun. The commercial cottons have a high proportion of lint to fuzz and the fibers themselves are white rather than brownish in color.

The wild *Gossypium* species that are known from Australia, Asia, Africa, and the Americas are perennial, drought-enduring shrubs and small trees that grow on the edges of deserts, in dry river beds, and on rocky hillsides. Cotton is known to have been cultivated and its fibers spun and woven as early as 4,500 to 5,000 years ago, both in Peru and in the Indus Valley of Asia.

Cultivated and wild species have been divided by taxonomists into seven groups according to their geographical, morphological, and chromosomal characters, all of which fit together rather well. Only two groups of wild species interest us now as resembling the ancestors of the cultivated cottons (which, themselves, fall into a third group).

In a widely accepted classification of the genus *Gossypium*, put forward in 1947 by Sir Joseph Hutchinson, section VII, *Herbacea*, includes two species that occur wild or semi-wild in the Old World tropics, and it is from them that the cultivated cottons of the Old World are derived. One of these species is *Gossypium arboreum*, a small tree that may have been developed in Asia from material brought in ancient times from Africa. In all probability, fibers from this species were the first to be spun in India. The second species, *Gossypium herbaceum*, is probably of African origin and may have been the first cultivated cotton of any sort. It is now widespread in Asia.

The cultivated Asiatic forms, compared with the wild ones, are more nearly annual in habit. Compared with the New World cultivated cottons, they have shorter lint and more fuzz hairs. Cytologically, they are characterized by having 13 pairs of large chromosomes. In genetics, these two sets of chromosomes are designated *AA* and, because the sets are two in number, the plants are said to be diploid.

Figure 4-8. Cotton (*Gossypium hirsutum*), showing leaves and flowers. From W. W. Robbins, *Botany of Crop Plants*. New York: McGraw-Hill Book Co., n.d. Reproduced by permission.

Figure 4-9. Leaves, unripe and ripe bolls (fruits), and seeds of cotton (*Gossypium hirsutum*). The lint fibers on one seed have been teased out; they have been removed from the other three seeds. Grown at University of California Botanical Garden.

The next section to be considered is section III, *Klotzschiana*. This includes species found wild in the Galapagos Islands, on the mainland of South America, and in Central and North America as far north as Arizona. One of the species in this section is *Gossypium raimondii*, from Peru. This species, although lintless (but still fuzzy), is believed (because of its other characters) to resemble one ancestor of the modern New World cultivated cottons. All species in this section are diploids with 13 pairs of small chromosomes, and these two sets of chromosomes are symbolized *DD*.

The third section to be considered is section VIII, *Hirsuta*. This contains the cultivated New World cottons, the major sources of cotton in the world today, whether from the southern states of the U.S., California, South America, or (transported to the Old World) the U.S.S.R., Egypt, and the Sudan. There are two cultivated species: *Gossypium hirsutum*, the so-called "American Upland" cotton, which is of Central American origin and has lint fibers approximately an inch long, and *G. barbadense*, the so-called "Sea Island" cotton or "Egyptian" cotton. The latter species appears to be a native of tropical South America, but was disseminated to the West Indies and from there was introduced into South Carolina and Georgia, whence its name "Sea Island" cotton. Since it is susceptible to infestation by the boll weevil, its growth is restricted to areas where this pest is not important. However, the lint on its seeds may reach as much as two inches in length.

Although *Gossypium hirsutum* and *G. barbadense* are almost certainly

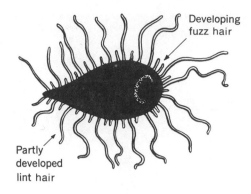

Developing
fuzz hair

Partly
developed
lint hair

Figure 4-10.   Diagrammatic side view of an immature cotton seed, showing differentiation between young fuzz hairs and lint hairs.

American in origin, it was believed until recently that they did not occur in a wild state. They exist in both perennial and annual forms and their special characteristic is that they are tetraploid. This means that they have 26 pairs of chromosomes—twice as many as the previously mentioned cottons. Thirteen pairs are large (*AA*) and 13 pairs are small (*DD*), so that the total chromosome complement is *AADD*.

The significance of these differences in chromosomes is that, since no cottons with only large chromosomes are known to come from the New World and no cottons with only small chromosomes are known to have grown in the Old World, the tetraploid cottons of the section Hirsuta presumably arose from the hybridization of a New World species with an Old World species followed by a doubling of the chromosome number. This hypothesis has been substantiated by recreating this hybrid and artificially doubling its chromosome number to produce a synthetic Hirsuta type.

It is still unknown how or when this cross occurred to give rise to our present-day tetraploid cultivated cottons. A modern origin is out of the question, since tetraploid species have been found at a number of archaeological sites in Peru. In fact, the oldest Peruvian remains, from the Chicama Valley, may date from 3000 B.C. This would make them comparable in age to that of the oldest recorded Old World cotton. Clearly, it could not have been the Portuguese or Spaniards who brought the two cottons together to hybridize in the New World, and we must conclude that the hybridization took place in pre-Columbian days.

If the hybridization took place in Asia, then both the diploid with the small chromosomes (*DD*) and the tetraploid (*AADD*) have since died out there, while the tetraploid would have had to migrate to the Americas before it died out in Asia. This is unlikely, and it is simpler to assume that the hybridization took place in the Americas.

If the diploid cotton with the *AA* chromosome sets emigrated naturally from the Old World, it has been generally assumed that it must have done so at a time in the past when there was a land connection. Transport of the seeds or fruits by sea currents was not seriously considered by botanists. Overland transport from Africa would have to have taken place before the separation of South America from Africa by sea floor spreading, while emigration from Asia would have to have been in the north across what is now the Bering Straits or in the south through Antarctica. However, it is doubtful if the climate in either of these last two regions was ever of the warm semi-desert type in which wild cottons thrive.

Consequently, a popular assumption was that some wandering human being from the Old World brought seed of a linted diploid cotton with him on a pre-Columbian visit to the New World and sowed it there. The descendants of the resulting plants could have persisted long enough to hybridize with a New World wild diploid cotton, producing an *AD* hybrid from which, by a doubling of the chromosome number, the *AADD* tetraploid arose. The Old World cotton, possibly because it was less valuable to people than the new tetraploid, might then have died out. Such a human contact could have been across the Atlantic Ocean or across the Pacific Ocean.

The situation is significantly changed, however, by archaeological evidence from southern Mexico, demonstrating that wild tetraploid cotton existed there before it was cultivated. *Gossypium hirsutum* has now been found wild on islands in the Caribbean as well as on the Mexican peninsula of Yucatan. *G. barbadense* occurs in apparently wild circumstances on the coasts of Ecuador and Peru, and the wild cotton of the Galápagos islands is now recognized to be a variety of this species (*G. barbadense* var. *darwinii*). There is a third New World species, *G. mustelinum* (also known as *G. caicoense*) growing wild in northeastern Brazil and possibly also in Colombia. All of this evidence suggests that human beings had nothing to do with the *origins* of tetraploid cotton, but that they domesticated *hirsutum* and *barbadense* separately in the New World.

In addition, S. G. Stephens, a geneticist who specializes in cotton, has shown that unopened bolls as well as the hard-coated seeds of the wild cottons float in seawater and retain their viability for an extended period. Thus, it is possible that diploid (*AA*) cotton seed could have drifted across one or other of the oceans from the Old World to the New World, perhaps at a time when Africa and the American continent were closer together than they are at present. The story of hybridization and chromosome doubling would remain the same as that already described, except that the dating is pushed back to a time before human beings were in the New World.

There is a fourth, unquestionably wild species in the section Hirsuta and, for a long time, it has been a thorn in the flesh of those who would maintain that human carriage is necessary to convey cotton across the oceans. This is

Gossypium tomentosum (*G. sandvicense*), which is restricted to the Hawaiian islands. Despite its short, brown, unusable lint, it appears to have a similar ancestry to that of *G. hirsutum* and, on these islands, is living testimony to the ability of a wild cotton to cross the ocean. It is probably derived from a wild ancestor in Mexico or Central America.

Stephens has emphasized that the cultivated cottons do not have the same powers of wide dispersal as the wild cottons — chiefly by reason of their thinner seed coats and the liability of their long lint-hairs to become interlocked, preventing the dispersal of the seed.

Although there are still some difficulties in interpreting the origin of the tetraploid cottons in the New World, at least we know how they crossed the Atlantic Ocean to Africa in more recent times to become important as "Egyptian" and "Sudan" cottons. In the eighteenth century, slave traders returning from the New World are known to have transported these better cottons to West Africa, where they showed their great superiority over the indigenous diploid cottons. In the nineteenth century, they were carried from West Africa by Arabs to the Sudan, Egypt, and Ethiopia. In the Sudan, in particular, they have displaced the shorter-linted diploids and have formed the basis of the cotton industry in the Gezira.

Summary

To sum up our discussion of possible pre-Columbian contacts between the Old World and the New World, we may say that the coconut and the gourd prove to be irrelevant. The peanut and maize were probably restricted to the New World in pre-Columbian times. The sweet potato probably demonstrates that some contact occurred, but that this was a limited one between South America and Polynesia. The history of cotton may indicate another limited contact between the Americas and Asia or Africa, but probably does not. Thus, on present evidence it can hardly be said that cultivated plants of the New World provide a foundation for the belief that there were any important cultural exchanges between the Americas and the Old World in pre-Columbian days. From the speed with which Old and New World crop plants were spread through the opposite hemispheres after 1492, it would seem that they would have been highly appreciated in earlier times by the people who did not have them.

5

Necessities:
Wheat

If we are to consider New World and Old World food plants separately, there is no more appropriate place to begin than with wheat (Fig. 5-1). Unquestionably of Old World origin, wheat is now the world's most widely cultivated crop, and is grown in all continents except Antarctica. Because of its extraordinarily widespread cultivation at the present day, there are wheat plants growing and maturing at all times of the year somewhere in the world. However, it is not everywhere that climatic conditions are suitable for wheat. As a crop it is grown most effectively in "grassland" climates with less than 30 inches of rainfall each year. In addition, wheat-growing climates must include a cold season; otherwise diseases will build up in the wheat populations.

Wheat is also one of the earliest cereals to have been brought into cultivation. The oldest known remains of cultivated wheat are grains of "Emmer" and "Einkorn," two distinct kinds of wheat, found at Tepe Ali Khosh in Iran and dating from before 7500 B.C. Nearly as old are remains from Turkey and Jericho in Jordan. Carbonized grains have been unearthed from the prehistoric village of Jarmo, a seventh-millennium-B.C. town in the Tigris-Euphrates basin (in what is now Iraq). The grains found at Jarmo match the grains of four kinds of wheat that are still extant: two are wild wheats (Wild Einkorn, *Triticum boeoticum* and Wild Emmer, *T. dicoccoides*), which still grow wild in the Near

Figure 5-1.   Comparison of a beardless (left) and a bearded (right) wheat.

East; the other two (Einkorn, *T. monococcum* and Emmer, *T. dicoccum*) are found nowadays only in cultivation.

The history of civilizations is bound up with the history of the cereals, and wheat is the cereal par excellence for breadmaking. Nevertheless, breadmaking is a relatively recent development in human culture — much more recent than the domestication of wheat. Before breadmaking, the grains were probably simply parched by heating. Primitive wheats had the grain firmly enclosed in husks or glumes, and heating makes it easier to rub off the glumes and allows the kernel to be more easily chewed or ground into meal.

A second stage in cultural development was probably that of grinding the parched grains and then soaking the coarse meal in water to make a gruel. Such gruel, after standing for a few days in a warm dwelling, would become infected with yeasts from the air. Fermentation would occur, producing a mild alcoholic beverage that would be useful in itself. It is possible that this process may also have pointed the way to the production of leavened bread by the making of fermented dough.

The Three Major Kinds of Wheat

Unlike maize, the wheat genus *Triticum* contains several cultivated species as well as wild ones, and all are products of the Old World. The Russian botanist N. I. Vavilov recognized 14 species of wheat; others have recognized more or less. The species fall into three groups, a division of the genus originally made in Germany in 1913 by Schultz on the basis of a combination of anatomical, morphological, and chemical properties. The chemical properties involved were particularly those that affected the baking properties of the flour.

In 1918 in Japan, Sakamura showed that the three groups differed in the number of their chromosomes. The first group contained 14 chromosomes (that is, two sets of 7); the second, 28 (4×7); and the third, 42 (6×7). Since the chromosomes are the bearers of genetic information from one generation to the next, it is of considerable scientific importance that these three groups of wheat species form such a series of chromosome numbers.

The 14-chromosome (diploid) wheats are basic to the series. The 28-chromosome group (the tetraploids) has arisen from the hybridization of the diploid wheats with other diploid grasses, followed by doubling in the number of chromosomes. By this means, new species can evolve suddenly. The 42-chromosome group (the hexaploid wheats) has arisen from the hybridization of tetraploid wheats with further diploid grasses, followed again by a doubling in the chromosome number of the hybrids. Since different wild grasses have been involved in the evolution of the wheats, the resultant species differ not only in the number of chromosomes but also in the genetic contents of those chromosomes. Nevertheless, three different sets of chromosomes, denoted A, B, and D, can be recognized in the various wheat species.

The 14-chromosome (diploid) wheats are probably the most ancient. There are two species: *Triticum boeoticum* ("Wild Einkorn") and *Triticum monococcum* ("Einkorn" — see Figs. 5-4 and 5-5). The name Einkorn ("one seed") derives from the fact that in both species each spikelet contains only one seed. Wild Einkorn is probably one ancestor of all the other cultivated wheats. In both species, the glumes remain clasped around the grain but the flower stalks are fragile. The tendency for the flower stalks to break aids the natural dispersal of the seed but results in losses during harvesting. Probably for this reason it was usual in ancient times for wheat to be harvested by grasping a cluster of stems in the hand and severing them high up (but beneath the point at which they are clasped) (Fig. 5-2). By this means, which is especially well illustrated on Egyptian tablets, the heads are subjected to the least amount of shaking and the fewest seeds are lost. However, because the glumes of Einkorn fit closely around the grain, giving it its firm-hulled character, it is difficult to use these diploid wheats for the preparation of human food. "Einkorn" seems to be simply a domesticated version of "Wild Einkorn," with slightly larger grains, and heads that do not fall apart quite as easily.

Both species of Einkorn have two sets of seven chromosomes that are similar in content; both are symbolized AA (Fig. 5-3). Wild Einkorn is native to the Near East and southeastern Europe; Einkorn appears to have originated from it in the Near East, although it spread as far as England by Neolithic (New Stone

Figure 5-2. Harvesting wheat in the Middle Ages. This wheat has fragile flower stalks; the stems must be held near the head while being cut.

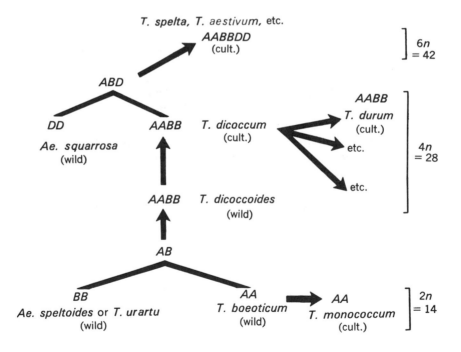

Figure 5-3. Simplified diagram of the history of diploid, tetraploid, and hexaploid cultivated wheats.

Age) times. The date of the first cultivation of Einkorn is unknown, but traces of it have been found in archaeological remains dating from the eighth millenium B.C.

Einkorn is still grown in the hilly regions of some parts of southern Europe and the Near East. Dark bread can be made from it, but, because of the difficulty of removing the glumes, it is usually used as whole grain for feeding cattle and horses.

The second group consists of the 28-chromosome or tetraploid wheats. Vavilov recognized seven species in this group, and they are apparently derived from the crossing of Wild Einkorn (*AA*) with a grass that is placed by many taxonomists in another genus, *Aegilops*. (Other botanists keep *Aegilops* and *Triticum* together as one genus under the latter name.) In all probability, the species involved was *Ae. speltoides* (Fig. 5-4), a diploid grass with two similar sets of chromosomes (*BB*). Crossing Wild Einkorn with *Ae. speltoides* gives a hybrid with the constitution *AB*. If by some accident the chromosome number was doubled, it would produce *AABB*, a fertile tetraploid (see Fig. 5-3). Very recently, another Near Eastern wild grass, *Triticum urartu,* was suggested as an alternative to *Aegilops speltoides* as the donor of the *BB* set of chromosomes to the tetraploid (and hexaploid) wheats.

One of Vavilov's seven tetraploid wheats is a wild plant. This is "Wild Emmer" (*Triticum dicoccoides*—Fig. 5-4), a species that occurs naturally in

Figure 5-4.   Left to right: Einkorn (*Triticum monococcum*), *Aegilops speltoides*, Wild Emmer (*T. dicoccoides*), Emmer (*T. dicoccum*), *Ae. squarrosa*, and Common Bread Wheat (*T. aestivum*). The fragile nature of the flower stalks in Wild Emmer is shown by the breaking away of spikelets.

the Near East. Closely related to Wild Emmer is the true Emmer (*T. dicoccum* — Fig. 5-4), which is known only from cultivation. Both Wild Emmer and the domesticated Emmer are present in very early archaeological remains, indicating that Emmer was domesticated from Wild Emmer more than 9,000 years ago. In fact, the tetraploid Emmer may have been cultivated as early as the diploid Einkorn.

Emmer was once the most widely grown of all wheats. It was the chief cereal of the Mediterranean region until the Graeco-Roman period, and, like Einkorn, has been found in Neolithic remains in the British Isles, a fact that shows how its use spread across the European continent in early times.

Good bread and fine pastry can be made from Emmer, but because it, too, has a fragile stem and clinging glumes, it is mostly fed to livestock in those places where it is grown nowadays. Other tetraploid wheats include Durum (*Triticum durum*), which is grown extensively in Italy, Spain, and the U.S. Because of its high gluten content, which makes it sticky when moistened, Durum is used to make macaroni, spaghetti, and semolina. The glumes of Durum do not enclose the ripe grain firmly, allowing it to be threshed free.

The 42-chromosome wheats, the hexaploids, consist of five species (unless these are considered to be simply subspecies of a single species, *Triticum aestivum* — see Figs. 5-1, 5-4, and 5-5). They are the most recently evolved of the wheats and are the most useful today, being the bread wheats. They are known only in cultivation. All of them are products of the hybridization of 28-chromosome wheats (*AABB*) with a diploid wild grass with the genetic constitution (*DD*), followed by doubling of the chromosome number. Thus, *AABB* × *DD* gives *ABD*; with a doubling of the chromosome number this gives *AABBDD*, a plant with six sets of seven chromosomes (see Fig. 5-3).

Actually, the grass with which the hybridization took place has been identified as another species of the genus *Aegilops, Ae. squarrosa* (see Fig. 5-4). This grass is sometimes referred to in recent literature as *Triticum tauschii*. It is a useless weed grass in wheat fields, ranging from the Balkans to Afghanistan. Consequently, it would have been present in tetraploid wheat fields of Asia Minor, in a good position to hybridize with the cultivated plant and produce a new kind of wheat that itself would be selected as a cultivated plant — a hexaploid wheat.

These steps in the evolution of wheat were almost certainly not made deliberately by man. He played a part in bringing the wheat parents and the weed grass parents into accidental contact, but natural hybridization made the next step, and, finally, man selected the product.

The most important hexaploid wheat is Common Bread Wheat, *Triticum aestivum* (otherwise known as *T. sativum* or *T. vulgare*). In the case of *Triticum aestivum* it is believed that the tetraploid parent was Persian Wheat (considered

---

Figure 5-5. Comparison of the sizes of heads of diploid *Triticum monococcum* (left) with hexaploid *T. aestivum* (right), illustrating the much greater yield of the latter.

by most taxonomists to be a variety of Emmer, *T. dicoccum*), which hybridized with *Aegilops squarrosa* prior to the doubling of the chromosome number. As a consequence, Common Bread Wheat probably originated in an area where Persian Wheat was grown, most likely northeastern Turkey or neighboring Russia. Unlike Emmer and the diploid wheats, the stalks of the inflorescence of this bread wheat are tough and do not shatter when the ear is harvested. On the other hand, the glumes open easily and allow the grain to fall out during the subsequent threshing process. Another hexaploid wheat, Spelt (*T. spelta*), has close-fitting glumes, and may have had a separate origin (probably from the hybridization of Emmer or Wild Emmer with *Aegilops squarrosa* followed by doubling of the chromosome number).

Bread wheats existed as early as 5000 B.C. in Iran, and are known from 2500 B.C. in India and from a roughly comparable date in Central Europe around the Neolithic lake dwellings. They have not been found anywhere as wild plants. Hexaploid wheats are now grown in all parts of the world from the tropics to the subarctic, with the greatest concentration in the temperate grassland regions. Their value lies in their productivity and in being easily threshed, as well as in the qualities of the gluten, the protein that produces a fluffy, leavened bread.

The Cultivation of Bread Wheat

Generally, the cultivated varieties of bread wheat can be divided into two groups — the spring wheats and the winter wheats. The spring wheats require a growing season of at least 100 days; they are generally sown in March and harvested in the fall, and can be grown in the colder regions of the world. The northern wheat belt of the U.S. and Canada is largely an area for growing spring wheats. The slower-growing winter wheats, on the other hand, must be raised in areas where fall rains are favorable and the winter is less severe. Consequently, the southern wheat belt of the U.S. is an area of winter-wheat growing. Here the grain is sown in September and is harvested the next July. As a compensation for the longer time of growth of this crop, it gives higher yields than the spring wheats.

Although man played only the role of a selector in the establishment of the hexaploid wheats as a grain crop, since the beginning of the twentieth century wheat has been given a great deal of attention by geneticists, who now play a vital role in breeding new varieties. In Europe and the U.S.A., the earlier programs of deliberate breeding were concerned with artificial hybridization and selection in order to bring together the most desirable characteristics of the existing strains, thereby combining good milling quality with strong stems and high yield. Now, when wheat yields are high and the quality is good, it is more important to produce disease-resistant strains of wheat, particularly strains with resistance to stem rust. Stem rust is due to the action of a fungus, *Puccinia graminis*, which is very widespread and very adaptable. It is probably the greatest cause of loss to wheat growers, except for unexpected unfavorable climatic conditions. The value of such a breeding program is strikingly illustrated by the success of the effort sponsored by the Rockefeller Foundation and the Mexican government to increase wheat production in Mexico. In 1943, when the program began, Mexico imported half of the wheat consumed in the country. However, in twenty years, from 1950 to 1970, there was an eightfold increase in wheat production in Mexico, partly due to increased wheat acreage but also stemming from a quadrupling of yield per unit area. This was achieved by concentrating first on the development of resistance to stem-rust disease (including the use of stem-rust resistant races of wheat developed in Kenya), and then by developing high yields through the utilization of crosses between the Mexican races and dwarf races developed in eastern Washington after being produced in Japan.

The use of dwarf wheats requires explanation. If a wheat plant has a tall but rather weak stem, it is liable to be beaten down and tangled with its neighbors during rain or in a high wind (a problem known as "lodging"). But increase in height of the stems is a natural reaction of plants which are given irrigation water and fertilizers. This treatment is desirable because it increases the yield of grain — and most Mexican wheat is grown in irrigated soils which need ferti-

---

lizers. Therefore, if an initially dwarf race of wheat can be used, the increase in height produced by the water and fertilizers does not lead to excessive "lodging." The dwarfs also produce more grain per plant, partly because there are more stems and partly because each stem bears more flowers.

To make their new races of wheat most productive on the farm, the Rockefeller and Mexican wheat specialists have also put into effect soil conservation measures, as well as demonstrations and farmer education programs. Attempts are now being made to see that small farmers, as well as the owners of large farms who can afford the necessary machinery and fertilizers, benefit from the use of the new methods and materials. The result of this international collaboration has been a virtual revolution in wheat production, and the task before agriculturists and politicians now is to bring the benefits of this revolution to all wheat growers.

The Future of Cultivated Wheat

Although the evolution of wheat, the most important of all crop plants, has been going on for thousands of years, the final picture is not visible. Indeed, it may be necessary for breeders to work continuously in order to keep wheat relatively free from disease, to increase the geographical range over which it may be grown, and to reduce the possibility that unfavorable climatic circumstances may completely eliminate a crop in any particular season over a wide area. Probably the greatest need in plant breeding at the present day is not the production of crop plants with greater potentialities of yield in favorable circumstances, but crop plants that will continue to give respectable yields even in unfavorable seasons. By this means, crop failures and famines that are their corollary may be banished from man's experience.

Following pioneer work in Canada and a development project carried on by Canadian and Mexican plant breeders working together, the first successful creation of a new cereal by crossing two distinct genera has been achieved. "Triticale" (*Triticosecale*), made by crossing wheat (*Triticum*) with rye (*Secale*) has been produced in hexaploid forms (with 42 chromosomes) and octoploid forms (with 56 chromosomes). The selected forms of Triticale that have come into production since 1970 combine the winter hardiness and resistance to rust disease of rye with the high yield and fine bread-making qualities of wheat. "Hybrid vigor" is apparent in the larger heads and grain size, and the protein content of the grain in these selected forms is higher than that of wheat.

6

Necessities:
Maize

Just as wheat was the characteristic cereal of the Old World, maize* was its counterpart in the New World, where there was no other cereal of comparable importance. Soon after the discovery of the New World, maize was introduced into the Old World, and has since become extremely important in the agricultural economies of all tropical, subtropical, and warm temperate regions of both Worlds. In exceptionally favorable circumstances, an acre of maize will yield more than 200 bushels of grain, compared to about 100 bushels for an acre of the highest yielding wheat.

The maize plant has a very characteristic structure (Fig. 6-1). Although it is an annual, it produces several tillers, so that more than one flowering shoot may be formed. Each shoot is supported at the base by a number of prop or adventitious roots developed from the lowermost nodes of the stem. The leaves, with their sheathing bases, are spread along the length of the stem. The mature stem is capped by a tassel containing the staminate flowers; pistillate flowers are borne laterally in ears. This separation of the pollen- and seed-producing flowers is unusual among grasses, and helps give maize its strikingly distinct appearance.

*Maize is used as a name in preference to corn because of possible confusion with the British use of corn as a name for wheat.

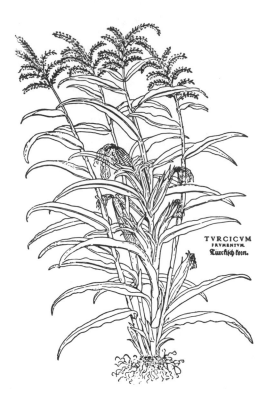

Figure 6-1. Maize (*Zea mays*). From Leonhart Fuchs, *De Historia Stirpium Commentarii Insignes*, 1542.

The ear of maize has, in itself, a very unusual structure, with no exact counterpart anywhere else in the plant kingdom. It represents a lateral shoot with very short internodes, which is subtended by one leaf; usually the ear bears up to seven leaves on a short, stout stem below the pistillate flowers. The pistillate flowers are crowded in rows along the "cob," and each one of the flowers produces a single grain (Fig. 6-2). While in the flowering condition, each of the one-seeded flowers produces a long silk, which is the stigma and style.

The endosperm in maize grains is a valuable source of starch, and some proteins, oils, and vitamins can be obtained from the aleurone layer and the embryo. Thus, maize grains can be extremely important in the human diet, whether directly or as food for domesticated animals. Unleavened bread and pancakes may be made from maize flour, though it cannot be used for leavened bread because of its inadequate gluten content. Grinding the endosperm of the grain into a powder produces cornstarch, which may be used for food or may be hydrolyzed to make corn syrup, a sugar syrup rich in glucose and of great value in the manufacture of babies' formulas. The embryo of the grain contains an oil that is used for cooking purposes and also in the manufacture of margarine, paint, and soap. The oil in the embryo constitutes up to six per cent of the weight of the grain.

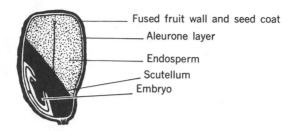

Figure 6-2. Diagram of longitudinal section through a maize grain.

The leaves, as well as the grain, can be used as a stock feed; in fact, in countries where the summers are too cool for the grain to ripen, it may still be worthwhile to grow maize in order to make silage from the leaves and stems, which have a high sugar content. It is advantageous if the tassels of male flowers can be included in this stock feed, because they are rich in vitamins. The pith from the stem makes a good, even-burning charcoal that is used in the fuses of explosives. Corn whiskey can be made from maize grains by breaking the starch down to sugar, followed by alcoholic fermentation by yeast and distillation to concentrate the alcohol.

History of Maize

Although maize first became known to the Old World in 1492, when it was discovered by two Spaniards sent by Columbus to explore the hinterland of Cuba, it was already long established as a crop plant in the New World. There is even evidence that it was in Mexico more than 5,000 years ago. In fact, all of the principal types of maize recognized today were already in existence in pre-Columbian times, and each one of these types is included in the same species, *Zea mays.*

Several general types of maize grains are recognized (Figs. 6-3 and 6-4). First, there is *popcorn* (Figs. 6-3a, 6-4a), whose grains swell and burst when heated, turning inside out. This "popping" is due to the fact that the center of the endosperm consists of cells with an unusually large proportion of water. They are surrounded by harder, drier tissue. On heating, the moisture in the cells in the center of the grain expands or turns to steam, thus building up pressure that ultimately explodes the grain so that it turns inside out.

The second kind of maize is *flour corn* (Figs. 6-3b, 6-4b). Here the "soft

---

(a)   (b)   (c)   (d)   (e)

Figure 6-3.   Left to right: (a) popcorn, with pointed grains; (b) flour corn, with variously colored grains (from Mexico); (c) flint corn; (d) an ear showing some grains with sugary endosperm (as found in sweet corn) which have shrunk on drying, the others being of the "dent" type; and (e) a modern "pod corn."

starch" in the cells of the endosperm easily forms a paste when ground and stirred with water. In flour corn the contents of the grain (that is, the one-seeded fruit) have a whitish color, except in some Middle American (from Mexico and Central America) and South American varieties where additional pigments give the grains a reddish or other color. Flour corn can be made more chewable by "parching" (heating for a short time over a fire).

The third kind of maize is *flint corn* (Figs. 6-3c, 6-4c). In this kind, the entire outer portion of the grain is composed of "hard" starch (which does not easily form a paste with water). This composition gives the grain a shiny surface. Flint corn can grow farther north than any of the other forms, and it is known that the Indians of the northeastern U.S. were growing a narrow-grained flint corn when the European settlers came.

Dent corn (Fig. 6-3d, 6-4d) is the fourth kind. Here the "hard" starch is confined to the sides of the grain. The "soft" starch forms the core and cap. "Soft" starch contracts when the grain is dried, producing the characteristic apical "dent." The dent characteristic of the grain is usually associated with high productivity, and most of the corn produced in the U.S. "corn belt" today is of this dent form and is largely used for livestock feeding. Nevertheless, the Indians in Virginia and the Carolinas were growing dent corn in pre-Columbian days.

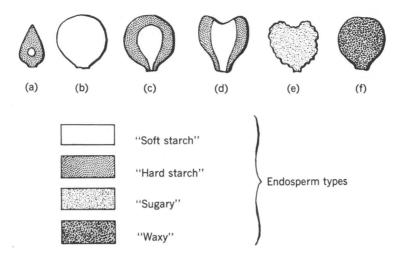

Figure 6-4. Diagrammatic sections through maize grains: (a) popcorn, (b) flour corn, (c) flint corn, (d) dent corn, (e) sweet corn, (f) waxy corn.

A fifth kind of maize still to be found today is *sweet corn* (Figs. 6-3d, 6-4e), in which the cells of the endosperm contain, in place of much of the starch, a rather high concentration of sugar. Sweet corn is usually harvested before it is ripe, while the endosperm is still liquid; it is then put to table use. When the grain of sweet corn is dried, it takes on a characteristically dark and shriveled appearance.

The last type, *waxy corn* (Fig. 6-4f), is a rare variety of maize. Usually, maize starch has two constituents — amylopectin and amylose. In waxy maize, however, the starch is made up of amylopectin only. Waxy maize may be used as a substitute for tapioca, which is made from the starch that occurs in the roots of the tropical cassava (*Manihot esculenta*).

An important form of maize that may have disappeared in its original state is *pod corn* (Fig. 6-3e). Its hereditary material turns up now and again in another form of maize, making it possible to recreate pod corn artificially. In pod corn, each grain is covered by small, leafy coverings called glumes, as is usually the case in grasses. Normally, in maize these glumes are present only in very reduced form as rudimentary sheaths at the base of each of the grains.

Maize is known today only in cultivation, although some 60,000-year-old pollen grains taken from a drill core some two hundred feet under Mexico City (made in preparing the foundations of a skyscraper) have been thought to belong to this species. In fact, in its present form, maize probably could hardly exist in the wild. The ears are covered by the large "husk" leaves, which would prevent the distribution of the grain. Also, if a cob should fall to the ground, its grains (which are firmly attached to the cob) could all germinate together, producing a competing mass of seedlings, and the likelihood is that none would reach maturity.

The usual procedure in trying to determine the origin of a cultigen is to look at the distribution of its nearest wild relatives. Consequently, much attention has been given to a Middle American plant that the Aztecs called *teocintl,* and which is now called *teosinte.* Its botanical name is in dispute because, while some botanists have thought it distinct enough from maize to warrant its placement in a separate genus (as *Euchlaena mexicana*), more modern treatments place it in the maize genus as *Zea mexicana* (or even as a variety of the maize species itself, as *Zea mays* var. *mexicana*).

Teosinte (Fig. 6-5b) is unquestionably a close relative of maize because both have ten pairs of chromosomes, and artificial hybrids between maize and teosinte are highly fertile. Also like maize, teosinte has separate pollen-bearing tassels and grain-bearing ears, the latter lightly wrapped in husk leaves, although there are far fewer grains to each ear of teosinte and each grain is enclosed in a hard "cupule." Teosinte grows as a wild or weed plant in Guatemala and Mexico, where there is much diversity among maize plants. This, then, is the sort of area that Vavilov would have approved as the center of origin of a crop, for here a putative wild relative is present and there is also much diversity in the crop plant itself.

However, many years ago, Edgar Anderson, after considering the morphology of the plants involved, suggested that teosinte might actually be derived from maize as a result of crossing with a species of *Tripsacum,* another genus of grasses. Anderson's suggestion led to the institution of genetical experiments, chiefly by P. C. Mangelsdorf and R. G. Reeves in Texas about 1930, in which maize was hybridized with teosinte and also with *Tripsacum.*

Tripsacum species have 18 pairs of chromosomes, and these chromosomes are strikingly different from those of maize. *Tripsacum* plants are also different in their outward morphology, having tasseled inflorescences bearing pistillate flowers at the base of the tassel and staminate flowers at the apex (Fig. 6-5c). Yet, from the partially fertile hybrids between these very dissimilar plants, further generations were raised, and some plants among them resembled teosinte in a number of characteristics. This caused Mangelsdorf to suggest that, rather than being an ancestor of maize, teosinte was derived from it. However, on various morphological and chromosomal grounds it is not now believed that teosinte had such an ancestry and it remains a contender for the title of maize's ancestor.

In attempting to detect the true ancestry of maize, it is important for investigators to be able to appreciate the changes that have taken place in maize itself since it first came into human hands. At the end of the nineteenth century, E. L. Sturtevant suggested that primitive maize was both a popcorn and a pod corn. Evidence in favor of this hypothesis was obtained by Mangelsdorf through

(a)   (b)   (c)

Figure 6-5. (a) Ear of corn; (b) ear of teosinte, *Euchlaena* (*Zea*) *mexicana*, with sheathing leaves; (c) terminal inflorescence of a species of *Tripsacum* with staminate flowers above and pistillate flowers below.

breeding and selection experiments starting with a modern form of pod corn (Fig. 6-3e). Through several generations of self-pollination, he carried out selection for characteristics that might have been seen in a wild or primitive maize. Lateral ears disappeared and pistillate flowers producing seeds appeared at the base of the tassel (compare Fig. 6-6). The tassels themselves are fragile, so that when they contain female flowers bearing seeds, these have a means of dispersal. Instead of being borne on a solid cob, the seeds are borne in an inflorescence that breaks up at maturity and distributes the individual grains (one-seeded fruits). Mangelsdorf pointed out that pod corn of this type could survive in the wild if it were able to grow and set seed there.

However, the first direct archaeological evidence as to the appearance of

Figure 6-6. Abnormal tassel of a maize plant bearing female flowers beneath the staminate ones.

primitive maize was discovered in the 1940s in an abandoned Indian rock cavern in New Mexico known as Bat Cave. There, in successive levels of the floor, are human remains, artifacts, and trash, dating from about 3500 B.C. to A.D. 1000. The oldest ears of maize (at the lowest level) are the smallest, have irregular rows of grains, and appear to have been a "podded" popcorn.

More recently, excavations by Dr. R. S. MacNeish in the floors of some caves in the valley of Tehuacán, about 150 miles south of Mexico City, have produced the first evidences of what could have been wild maize, dating from about 5000 B.C. The tiny ears, less than an inch in length, bear only a couple of husk leaves. The brownish, round grains show the remains of relatively long glumes and are borne on fragile "cobs" (providing a means of seed dispersal). The ears are tipped with the remains of staminate inflorescences but apparently were borne just below the tassel. No cultivated plants are present in this layer of the cave floor, giving credence to the idea that this maize was collected in the wild.

Not all students of the history of maize accept the view that this maize was wild, and there is a growing body of opinion that it had already been influenced by human selection. It is the view of maize specialist Walton C. Galinat and geneticist George Beadle that maize, as such, never existed in the wild and that it was selected by human beings out of teosinte (which would have been more variable then than now).

Galinat and Beadle point to the chromosomes of maize and teosinte, which are identical in number (but differ from those of *Tripsacum*). Furthermore, the fine structure of the chromosomes of maize and teosinte agree closely. Analysis of the composition of seed proteins (by the process known as electrophoresis) similarly shows agreement, as does the morphology of the pollen grains. Beadle has been able to show by genetical studies that only five mutations would be needed to account for the basic differences between teosinte and a popcorn maize. A few more mutations could be responsible for the increase in number of grains on the cob. Teosinte could have been a human food for its grain can be "popped" like popcorn.

As yet, there is no archaeological evidence for the theory that the domestication of teosinte represents the manner in which maize evolved, and it must be recorded that there are still those that believe both in the reverse relationship— that teosinte is a derived, weedy form of maize (although not by hybridization with *Tripsacum*) — and in the common ancestor relationship — that maize and teosinte have been derived separately from a common ancestor, presumably long extinct.

It is perhaps surprising that, although maize is one of the world's most important food sources and more is known of its genetics than of any other plant, its ancestry should be shrouded in so much mystery. However, this is a feature of many of the most valuable plants in our economy—they were among the first to be domesticated and have been the most intensively selected during their long histories.

Hybrid Corn

Although we are not certain about the ancestry of maize, its recent history has been carefully documented. It is with maize that the greatest triumphs of plant-breeding have been attained during the last quarter of a century. During this period, the development of "hybrid corn" has revolutionized agriculture in the American corn belt, and this revolution is now spreading to the rest of the world. Actually, all maize is hybrid in the sense that it is normally cross-pollinated, but "hybrid corn" is a special kind of carefully produced hybrid.

Plants that are normally cross-pollinated can, in many cases, be self-pollinated, but if this practice is actually carried out and is continued for several generations, the resulting plants are liable to show "inbreeding depression." Figure 6-7 indicates the course of events over a number of generations, showing the period of inbreeding depression followed by one of stabilization at a rather low level of vigor.

When plants from two such inbred lines are crossed, however, the resulting hybrid is likely to exceed in vigor even the original progenitors of the inbred lines (Fig. 6-7). This production of "hybrid vigor" was first investigated experimentally by Charles Darwin in the middle of the nineteenth century.

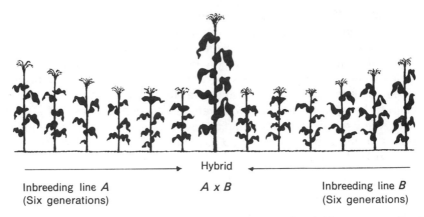

	Hybrid	
Inbreeding line *A* (Six generations)	*A* x *B*	Inbreeding line *B* (Six generations)

Figure 6-7. Purification of two lines of maize by inbreeding (with accompanying "depression" in vigor until a stable condition is reached) followed by crossing of the two pure lines to produce an exceptionally vigorous hybrid. This is the "single-cross" method for hybrid corn production.

Darwin published his results and also described them in letters to Asa Gray, the great American botanist at Harvard University.

Gray had a student named William Beal, who later became a professor at Michigan State College, where he worked on the utilization of hybrid vigor to increase the yield of maize. He took two varieties and grew them in a field isolated from other maize varieties. Then he removed the unopened tassels from every plant of one variety so that the pistillate flowers from the detasseled plants set seed by cross-pollination from the variety that had not been detasseled. When these crossbred seeds were harvested and planted the next season, the resultant hybrid plants grew vigorously.

Because Beal used two unselected and therefore impure varieties, his results were not fully repeatable, and, for this reason among others, his system was not generally adopted by commercial producers of maize seed. The next step was taken by George H. Shull, working at the Cold Spring Harbor Laboratories, near New York. Shull added the needed extra touch, that of purity in the parents, and achieved uniformity in the hybrid product. This purity in the parents was obtained by inbreeding the parental lines for several generations. Figure 6-7 shows the process involved, and also makes evident that only the first hybrid generation would be used for commercial corn production.

Unfortunately, Shull's idea that commercially unproductive inbred lines of the potential parents should be grown simply to produce a vigorous hybrid product did not appeal to farmers and took a long time to catch on. Furthermore, because the inbred strains used as seed-parents produced only small ears bearing small numbers of grain, hybrid seed obtained by this method — the so-called "single-cross" method — was too expensive for ordinary purposes.

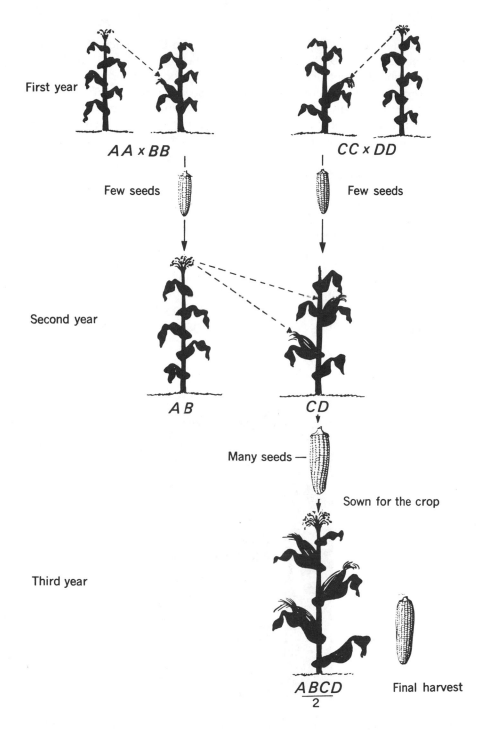

Figure 6-8. Stages in the production of "single-cross" ($A \times B$) and "double-cross" ($A \times B$) $\times$ ($C \times D$) hybrid corn.

The next step was made by Donald Jones at the Connecticut Agricultural Experiment Station in 1918. Jones introduced the "double-cross" method, in which four inbred strains are combined. This method involves two crossings, which require two seasons before the ultimate seed is produced. This ultimate seed is then sown to give the commercial crop of maize in the third season. However, as Fig. 6-8 indicates, the desired hybrid seed is produced in vastly increased numbers by this means because, although seed from the first cross is produced on small ears borne by dwarfed, inbred plants, seed from the second cross is produced on large ears borne by large "single-cross" plants. However, the seed produced from such a "double-cross" is genetically less uniform than that produced in each "single-cross," and there has been a tendency in commercial maize growing to return to the use of "single-crosses" using more vigorous inbred lines.

Hybrid maize (Fig. 6-9) has vastly increased the yield of grain per acre but has put upon the farmer the need to buy new hybrid seed each year. However, the large, highly organized industry that supplies it has the capacity to produce hybrid seed tailored (by crossing appropriate inbred lines) to the climatic, soil, and marketing conditions prevailing in each area where the crop will be grown.

Figure 6-9. (Left) Ear of "flint corn" from a North American Indian source. (Right) Ear of "hybrid corn." Note increase in numbers of rows and grains per row. The grains have the dent characteristic.

The techniques developed for producing hybrid maize have been extended to the production of other economically important crops. Thus, much hybrid sorghum, and many hybrid onions and sugar beets are now produced on the farms of the U.S.A. In all these crops, including maize, the hybrids are produced by the "male-sterility" method. For each species, races have been developed containing a gene that causes a failure of pollen production. These races, if grown in the presence of a normal pollen-fertile race, set their seed by cross-pollination from the latter race (Fig. 6-10). In the cases of sorghum and maize, where the seed of the next generation is the desired crop, it is arranged that the pollen from the pollen-fertile parent also carries a "fertility-restoring" gene so that the hybrid plants, when they are grown, are capable of forming pollen for the production of their own seed. In the case of onions and beets, where underground parts are harvested, it is not necessary (or even desirable) for the hybrid crop to set seed.

So successful has this male-sterility method of producing hybrid crops become that the technique is being used experimentally in the production of "hybrid wheat," as well as many other crops. But it has its dangers if it leads to a narrowing of the genetic base for the crops. Thus, by the late 1960s, almost all hybrid maize produced in North America was based on crosses involving the same male-sterility gene (producing so-called "Texas cytoplasmic male-sterility"). In the winter of 1969–70 and the summer of 1970, the susceptibility of all hybrids with this gene to a disease caused by a mutant form

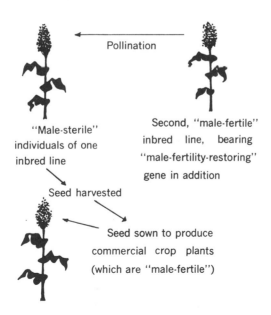

Figure 6-10. Theoretical basis of the "male-sterility" method of producing hybrid sorghum and other crops.

of the southern corn leaf blight fungus (*Helminthosporium maydis*) was dramatically demonstrated by an epidemic of the disease which swept through North America from Florida to Canada. Huge losses were sustained and action was called for to utilize different genes for male sterility in the production of future hybrids. The danger of genetic uniformity in crop plants that was revealed reminds one of the lesson that should have been learned from the Irish potato famine (Chapter 3, page 41).

7

Luxuries:
Sugar

Sugars are the simplest kinds of carbohydrates. The commonly encountered sugars may be divided into (1) two kinds of monosaccharides: hexoses, such as glucose and fructose, with the empirical formula $C_6H_{12}O_6$, and pentoses, with the formula $C_5H_{10}O_5$; and (2) disaccharides, generally with the formula $C_{12}H_{22}O_{11}$, and including sucrose (or cane sugar) and maltose (or malt sugar). Sucrose is formed from the condensation together of a glucose and a fructose unit with the elimination of a molecule of water; maltose is made from the similar condensation together of two glucose units. The continued condensation together of sugar molecules produces increasing molecular complexity, leading eventually to the production of polysaccharides such as the dextrins, starches and cellulose.

Sugars are important because they are the primary carbohydrate products of photosynthesis, and can be respired by both plants and animals to provide energy; they also serve as the basis for construction of more complicated molecules in plant tissues. For man, they are luxuries compared with more complex carbohydrates, which provide a more compact meal that can be broken down inside one's body to release the sugars. Starchy foods are also more easily stored than sugary ones.

The earliest source of sugar for human consumption was honey, and this is still collected all over the world where honey bees are found (Fig. 7-1). Honey is made by bees from the nectar of flowers, and it usually contains glucose, fructose and sucrose. Honey bees are not native in North America; they were introduced into the country from Europe, and have since spread and become thoroughly naturalized.

Until the early eighteenth century, the European man-in-the-street had no sweetening substance other than honey, although since Roman times sugar had been brought into Europe from Asia as an expensive import. Like so many exotic substances, it was carried to Europe from India by overland Arab caravans. The Romans knew it to have been extracted from a "bamboo-like grass." This grass, however, needed abundant moisture for its growth, and the arid countries between India and the Mediterranean region prevented the Arabs (even if they had been willing) from bringing the plant itself to Europe and the Middle East. Consequently, sugar was a rare commodity in Europe until the end of the Middle Ages, and was used only by the aristocracy. It was sold in apothecaries' shops as a medicine (a sedative).

Figure 7-1. Woman gathering honey, Spanish Mesolithic cave art. From C. S. Coon, *The History of Man*, London: Jonathan Cape, 1955. Reproduced by permission.

Sugar Cane

The sugar extracted in India came from the sugar cane (*Saccharum officinarum*) (Fig. 7-2), which is probably native to southeastern Asia. Although sugar cane is not known as a wild plant, about 12 other species of the same genus occur in a natural state in tropical Asia, and at least five of these are native to India. Cultivated sugar cane is probably not a pure species, but is derived from hybridizations between at least two species, and may have been

Figure 7-2. Sugar cane (*Saccharum officinarum*), showing jointed stem stripped of leaves. A waxy deposit partially covers the stem. Photograph by W. H. Hodge from Ward's Natural Science Establishment, Inc. Reproduced by permission.

subjected, later in its history, to further hybridization with other wild species. Sugar cane belongs to the same tribe of grasses as sorghum, which itself has a fairly high sugar content and has also been used to produce sugar.

Sugar cane is a tall, very obviously jointed grass with a solid stem reaching as much as 10 or even 15 feet in height. A single plant produces a number of stems in a tuft from ground level, where they are supported by prop roots. The stem is topped by a feathery white inflorescence, but this produces few seeds and the cane is normally propagated by vegetative means. The explanation of the rare seed setting by sugar cane seems to lie in its hybrid origin and in its very high and variable chromosome number. In addition, its pollen grains and seeds have only a very short life.

The plant is propagated by planting "sets" cut from the upper part of the stem of an old cane. Each "set" contains several nodes and internodes of the stem and is about eight to ten inches long. The uppermost nodes in the sets produce new shoots from axillary buds; the lowermost nodes produce rings of adventitious roots (Fig. 7-3). The shoots grow until the terminal bud is used up in the formation of an inflorescence, after which, unless the cane is har-

---

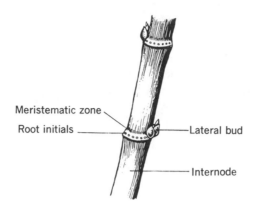

Meristematic zone
Root initials
Lateral bud
Internode

Figure 7-3. Portion of stem of sugar cane. From L. S. Cobley, *An Introduction to the Botany of Tropical Crops*. London: Longmans, Green & Co., 1956. Reproduced by permission.

vested, the shoot will die. Under favorable conditions, a "set" can continue to produce aerial stems for as many as 20 years, but on poorer soils the length of life of a plant is much less.

The cane is harvested by chopping it off at the base, and the sugar-rich juice is pressed out by passing the cane through rollers. Several passages may be necessary, with wetting of the cane between each passage. This extraction of the juice is a relatively recent development in man's history; in the past, the cane was usually chewed raw, and is still enjoyed this way by many people in the tropics.

When the juice is extracted, it is evaporated, and the sugar is refined, losing many of its impurities in the process. Actually, some of these "impurities" are valuable in a healthful diet but are lost to the more civilized consumer. After evaporation, the liquid may be centrifuged, whereupon the solid portion that is obtained is crystalline brown sugar (while the remaining liquid forms molasses). The molasses may be further evaporated or used as a cattle feed; in the West Indies, molasses is fermented and distilled to produce rum. In other parts of the world it is fermented into vinegar. Sugar may be further refined and decolorized with activated charcoal to produce white sugar, which is almost completely pure cane sugar or sucrose.

Most sugar cane is grown between 30° north and south of the Equator—in Cuba and other Caribbean islands, Brazil, the Philippines, Hawaii, India, and Java. However, the greatest consumption of sugar is in temperate lands. Consequently, the geographical gap between the producing and consuming regions is of considerable importance, especially in Europe, and particularly in wartime. Therefore, it is not surprising that through the ages there have been searches for substitute sources of sugar for human consumption.

Sugar Beet

Most conspicuously useful among these substitute sources of sugar is the swollen "tap root" of the sugar beet (*Beta vulgaris*) (Fig. 7-4, left). Actually, the upper portion of this "root" consists of tissue that is technically hypocotyl. About a third of the sucrose produced in the world today comes from this source. The sugar beet belongs to the family Chenopodiaceae, which is largely made up of plants growing in salty places, on sea coasts, and on saline soils in desert regions. The sugar beet is no exception to this, having been derived by domestication from a European seashore plant, *Beta maritima*, which was

Figure 7-4. (Left) A flowering plant of the garden beet. (Right) a vegetative plant of chard. Both are forms of *Beta vulgaris*, the species that also includes the mangel-wurzel and the sugar beet. Grown at University of California Botanical Garden.

---

first domesticated for its greens, and then later, by selection, for its edible tap roots. In fact, selection within this one species has produced at least four quite distinct economic plants—chard, mangel-wurzel, the garden beet, and the sugar beet.

Chard (Fig. 7-4, right) does not have a very swollen root but is important for its foliage, which is eaten as greens. In the mangel-wurzel, the root is extremely important. It is yellowish-white in color and is used for cattle feed. Thirdly, there is the garden beet, which is usually eaten cooked and often pickled in vinegar. The forms of garden beet with deep red roots are definitely known only since the sixteenth century, and, of course, are notable not only for their pigment content but also for their sweet taste. Unquestionably, it was this sweetness that gave the clue to the use of this species as a source of sugar.

Consequently, we have the fourth kind of beet, the sugar beet, first envisaged as a crop in Germany at the end of the eighteenth century and then developed by intensive selection in the early part of the nineteenth century by a plant breeder named Achard. This beautiful example of the application of selection techniques in the days before the laws of heredity had been discovered has increased the sugar content of whiterooted beets from approximately two per cent to about 20 per cent. Few inventions prosper without publicity, and in the case of sugar beet the new crop was promoted by Napoleon I, who recognized the advantage of having a home-grown source of sugar in the part of war-torn Europe that was under French control. Over a century later, in both world wars, sugar beets proved to be of very great value to all European countries. In the United States, sugar beet has been grown commercially only since about 1875, but it is now a very important crop in many northern and western states, particularly California. Prolonged high temperatures reduce the sugar content in the root, and this limits the areas where sugar beets can be grown.

Beta vulgaris is a biennial plant. The seed is sown in rows in spring and, after germination and some growth, these are thinned mechanically. By midautumn the whitish cylindrical or conical roots, which weigh up to six pounds each, are ready for harvesting. Any plants needed to produce seeds are also taken up and are stored during the winter. They are planted again in the spring, and they flower in their second summer, producing greenish, wind-pollinated flowers on stems three to four feet high (Fig. 7-4, left).

The sugar is extracted from the beets by shredding them and soaking the shreds or "cossettes" in hot water. This process, which is carried on in large factories usually situated in the producing area, removes the great majority of the sugar. The wet, shredded material may be pressed to remove the small amount of sugar that remains. The beet pulp that is left after this process may be used as a source of pectin, as livestock feed (though it is poor in protein), or even as a fertilizer. The sugar solution is purified in the same manner as the solution that is derived from sugar cane.

Minor Sugar Sources

Yet another source of sugar is from trees. It has already been mentioned that sugar can be obtained from the sap of palms. Nevertheless, there is also a temperate source of sugar from trees. This source is the sugar maple, *Acer saccharum*, a tree belonging to the family Aceraceae. Although many maple trees yield a sugary sap, only the sugar maple does so in sufficient quantity and with a high enough sugar content to justify its exploitation.

The sugar maple was known to the Indians of northeastern North America, and sap extraction was practiced there before the arrival of the white man. It can only be done in early spring, when "the sap begins to run." At this time, the starch reserves in the wood of the roots and trunk are converted into sugar and are carried in solution in the sap. Between February and April, tests are made on the trees. When these tests show that the sap is moving upwards, a hole about two inches deep is bored in the trunk, a short metal tube is inserted in the hole, and the sap is allowed to drip through it into a covered bucket. Even though the sugar maple is the richest North American source of sugar, only five per cent of its sap is actually sugar (sucrose). The sap is boiled down to produce maple syrup; further boiling results in a thick paste, which, on cooling, solidifies into maple sugar.

Sugar is also produced from various cereal plants. In the United States, certain varieties of sorghum are grown for sugar production, the sap being pressed out of their stems as in sugar cane. More important, however, is the production of sugar by hydrolysis of the starch in maize grains. This process, which is carried out under the influence of dilute acid, produces so-called corn syrup. There is a difference here, however, in that corn syrup is very rich in glucose, in contrast to all of the other commercially important plant-sugar products, which consist almost entirely of sucrose.

Unlike starch, sugar is a luxury. It is not essential for human food to be sweetened, and, indeed, for a large proportion of the world's population there is no sweetening. But the addition of sugar to our diet has converted eating from a mere necessity to a great pleasure. As is usual in the history of cultivated plants, however, there is a tendency for synthetic chemicals to replace some of their functions. At least some of the sweetening function of sugar, for example, is taken over by synthetic chemicals such as saccharin which, as long as they have no side effects, can be used to sweeten foods and drinks and do not have sugar's energy- (or weight-) producing proclivities. They are important to people who suffer from diabetes. Even some naturally occurring plant chemicals are much sweeter than sugar. Thus the so-called "serendipity berries," the fruits of *Dioscoreophyllum cumminsii* (Menispermaceae) contain a protein called monellin that is 3,000 times sweeter than sucrose. Other intensely sweet substances occur in the berries of the West African herbaceous plant, *Thaumatococcus danielli* (Marantaceae) and in the leaves of *Stevia*

---

rebaudiana (Compositae) from South America. Also, grapefruit peel apparently contains a bitter substance that can be chemically converted into a sweetener (see also Chapter 15, page 182).

Some years ago, E. C. Large, in a novel called *Sugar from the Air*, attempted to describe the changes in man's life that would result from the artificial production of sugar from carbon dioxide and water under the influence of solar radiation but without the involvement of green plants. This novel may be recommended for reading, but it should also be remembered that, although this process has been carried out in the laboratory, it is unlikely to become economically feasible for a long time. When the capture of solar energy in edible form does become practicable, however, this process may be the harbinger of a revolution of the greatest importance to mankind.

8

**Necessities Again:
Legumes and Oils**

Legumes

In addition to carbohydrates, the human diet must contain fats and proteins. Proteins, however, are often in short supply. Even in the tropics, where cereals may be infrequently grown, starches are generally available in such staples as cassava, taro, and yams. But there is often a protein deficiency in the diet of the indigenous peoples, particularly in the more densely populated regions of the world. For primitive man, the supply of proteins was no great problem; he was a hunter, and animals provided him with proteins. But as the human population increased and as man changed from a nomadic hunting system to a settled agricultural one, it became necessary for plants to furnish a greater proportion of his protein intake.

In a more vegetarian diet, leguminous plants are rich sources of proteins. These plants belong to the family Leguminosae (Fabaceae) and produce a fruit (a legume) with a very characteristic structure. It is a capsular pod that opens along two lines of dehiscence when ripe. Most economically important plants of this family also have a characteristic butterfly-shaped flower (Fig. 8-1).

The richness of leguminous plants in protein can be attributed, in part, to their special methods of nitrogen nutrition. Usually, plants of this family bear nodules on their roots. These nodules contain bacteria, generally classified in the genus *Rhizobium*, which can live free in the soil but are of greater importance when they enter the roots of the plants, since there they have the power of turning (or "fixing") atmospheric nitrogen into useful amino acids, which are the building blocks of proteins. The bacteria receive carbohydrates and other nutritive substances from the host plant, and this may be looked upon as an example of mutualism. One important consequence of this relationship is that leguminous plants can grow in soils that are deficient in natural nitrates, and, if the remains of these plants are plowed in after the pods and seeds have been harvested, the soil can be enriched significantly. Consequently, for a long time, leguminous plants have had a place in crop rotations.

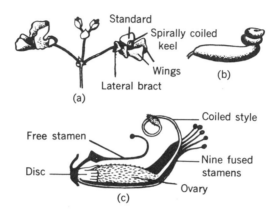

Figure 8-1. Structure of the flower of the common bean (*Phaseolus vulgaris*), representing the Leguminosae. (a) Inflorescence. (b) Spirally twisted "keel" of two petals. (c) Longitudinal section through flower after removal of petals and sepals. From L. S. Cobley, *An Introduction to the Botany of Tropical Crops*. London: Longmans, Green & Co., 1956. Reproduced by permission.

Proteins are composed of amino acids condensed together. Specific amino acids are needed to make the proteins which are essential for human life. Three of these—lysine, methionine, and tryptophan—are among those that cannot be manufactured from others within the human body and must be present in the diet; however, they are deficient in many plant protein sources, particularly cereal proteins. They can be supplied by adding leguminous plant materials to the food. It was no coincidence that the Indians of the American tropics and subtropics settled on a balanced diet predominantly consisting of maize (corn) and beans (which are the seeds of certain leguminous plants). Nor is it surprising that the combination of rice and beans is so widely used now. Recently, plant breeders at Purdue University produced a race of maize, "opaque-2," which contains twice as much lysine and more tryptophan than is usually found in maize corn.

Most leguminous crop plants are warm-season annuals. Even the scarlet runner bean (*Phaseolus coccineus*), which is a perennial, is usually grown as an annual plant. The seeds of leguminous plants (Fig. 8-2) are often quite large and are mostly filled by the two cotyledons of the embryo plant, with a tiny root and shoot system between them. The plants may be harvested when the seeds are ripe and the pod is dry, as in the case of peas and the larger beans, or the whole pod containing the seeds may be harvested in an immature condition, as in various kinds of string beans. The edible seeds and fruits of leguminous plants are generally referred to as "pulses."

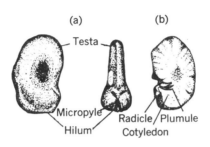

Figure 8-2. Seed of broad bean (*Vicia faba*). (a) Two exterior views and (b) view of the embryo with one cotyledon removed.

The seeds of legumes form a rich source of food and, because of their low water content, they are easily stored. Consequently, they have been valued from early times in both the Old and New Worlds. However, there has been a much greater development of leguminous crop plants in the New World, and at least nine species of the genus *Phaseolus* were widespread throughout the Americas before 1492. Four of these species are most important. They are the common bean (*Phaseolus vulgaris*), the tepary (*P. acutifolius* var. *latifolius*), the sieva or lima bean (*P. lunatus*), and the scarlet runner bean (*P. coccineus*). Of these, the common bean may have been the first to be domesticated, with remains dating from 4975 B.C. from the Tehuacán Valley in Mexico and possibly even earlier from Peru. It may have been domesticated several times in different regions of Middle and South America. Similarly, the lima bean was probably domesticated separately in Middle America and in Peru. Remains of lima beans and common beans have been found in an Andean valley in Peru and dated at 6000 B.C., while fragments of both species, as well as beans of the genus *Canavalia,* have been recognized in dried human excreta (coprolites) unearthed in coastal Peru dating from almost 3000 B.C. Wild *Phaseolus* beans contain poisonous glycosides which liberate hydrocyanic acid when chewed; the reduction or elimination of these substances is one of the changes in the plants which have accompanied domestication.

Because all the native Old World cultivated species of *Phaseolus*,* such as mung, adsuki, and gram beans, have small seeds, the large-seeded New World beans were welcomed when they were carried to the Old World. The peanut, *Arachis hypogaea*, already discussed, is another valuable leguminous seed of New World origin which has been welcomed by the Old World.

Soybeans

One of the most exciting stories is that of a legume that originated in the Old World—one that was brought into cultivation in ancient times but has become widespread only rather recently. This is the soybean (*Glycine max*) (Fig. 8-3). The genus *Glycine* contains between 30 and 50 species of low-growing, often twining shrubs and herbs, generally distributed through Asia. The soybean itself is not known as a wild plant, but a wild species in eastern Asia (*G. ussuriensis*) is so much like it that it is probably its ancestor, unless both species arose from a common ancestor.

We have historical evidence that the soybean has been cultivated in China for centuries, undergoing cultivation there even before written records were kept. Its cultivation gradually spread from China through Russia, and the soybean became well established in eastern and southern Europe. It never became very popular in Africa, but during the twentieth century it spread to South America. It took longer to achieve recognition in North America, where it was not produced commercially until 1924. However, North America now produces over 60 per cent of the world's soybean output, so important has this plant become now that its virtues have been recognized.

Because of its long history in cultivation and because of the intensive breeding work that has been carried out with it recently, thousands of varieties of soybean are now known. These are adapted to various uses and to the diversity of environments in which the plants may be grown. Although U.S. production of soybeans is centered in Illinois, varieties adapted to growing conditions all the way from Canada to Louisiana have been selected. The plants vary from two to six feet in height, and usually are erect or even twining (see Fig. 8-3). The flowers vary in color from nearly white to deep purple, and the pods they produce may be from one to three and a half inches in length. The seeds range from white to red, brown, and black; their oil and protein contents also vary significantly.

Although such variability is true of the species as a whole, any particular population may be extremely uniform in all of these characteristics. This is because pollen is usually shed from the stamens onto the stigma before the flowers open, and thus self-fertilization usually occurs, tending to produce genetically pure lines.

---

* Now often placed in the closely related genus *Vigna*.

Figure 8-3. Shoot of a soybean plant (*Glycine max*), showing leaves and fruits.

The ancient Chinese and today's inhabitants of the tropics and the Far East put the soybean to use as a pulse, largely valued for its high protein content, although it is also rich in oil and high in calcium, iron and vitamins.

The beans may be used fresh in salads or they may be roasted and eaten like peanuts. Sprouted beans are used in making chow mein. More recently, soybean oil has become important in the manufacture of cooking fats, margarine and other food products, and in soaps, glycerine, and linoleum. It is also mixed with other oils for a variety of uses in the paint and varnish industries, and is valuable for making putty, waterproofing material, lubricants, and leather dressings. The oil is usually expressed under pressure or obtained by continuous solvent extraction.

The residue after most of the oil has been expressed is called soybean meal or flour, and has a protein content ranging from 40 to 50 per cent of its dry weight. Because it contains an inhibitor of the enzyme trypsin (which digests protein in the human intestine), soybean flour must be specially treated to destroy this inhibitor before it can be consumed in large amounts. But, once this has been done, there is apparently no limit to the number of items that can be made from soybean flour for consumption by human beings and domesticated animals!

Soybean flour has become increasingly important as a direct constituent of prepared food mixes (especially where its strong flavor can be disguised with some other flavor), and it is to be found particularly in breakfast foods, bread, muffin mixes, some "non-dairy creamers," and a number of dog and cat foods.

Necessities Again: Legumes and Oils

An ancient use for soybean flour is in the manufacture of soy sauce. By contrast, its use to provide the protein in "meat analogues" and "extenders" is very recent. These imitations of meat sausages, hamburger beef, and bacon slices are produced by extracting the protein from soy flour, mixing it with mucilage (also from a plant source), and extruding the viscous liquid through a spinnaret into a coagulating bath. Colorings, flavorings and various other nutrients are added, and the protein threads are woven or matted into "meat." With appropriate additives, a nutritionally balanced foodstuff can be prepared, with the additional dietary advantage of being cholesterol-free.

Soybean flour can be used to make soy curds and soy cheese under bacterial influence. In addition, it has innumerable industrial uses in the manufacture of adhesives, sizings, plastics, printing inks, insecticides and synthetic textiles. Soybean plants may also become an important source of sapogenins for drug manufacture (see Chapter 13). After the beans have been harvested, the plants may serve as forage for domesticated animals or be plowed into the soil as a green manure.

Thus, the soybean plant is an unusual example of a contemporary economic plant with multiple uses. It is very important that a tropical equivalent of the temperate zone soybean is now attracting the attention of agriculturists. This is the winged bean (*Psophocarpus tetragonolobus*) from southeast Asia (see Chapter 15, page 178).

Forage Legumes

Most leguminous plants do not have the soybean's multitude of uses; however, it would be very difficult to imagine life without them for, in addition to their direct contribution to our diet, they also contribute indirectly in large measure. It is difficult to think of livestock pastures not containing various sorts of clover or other leguminous plants and the most valuable of all prepared animal feeds is made from alfalfa (*Medicago sativa*). Most of the important temperate forage leguminous plants are of Old World origin, but this is not surprising when we remember that the Indians of the New World lacked herbivorous domesticated animals. Furthermore, alfalfa itself could not be successfully grown in some parts of the New World, particularly in the northwest, before the Old World honey bee was introduced, or, better still, before the large native "alkali bee" was encouraged to increase its numbers by the provision of artificial nesting sites in the banks around the fields. These relatively large bees are needed to pollinate the flowers and enable them to set seed.

Oil Sources

The soybean has provided us with an unusual example of a plant that is valuable for both its protein and its oil content. Most plants that are grown as sources of oils or fats, however, are single-purpose crop plants. As a result of metabolic activities, parts of a plant build up food reserves in the form of oils or fats. In particular, oils and fats are found in seeds, where they are made from sugars that have been translocated there. Fats and oils are chemically similar substances in different physical states. Fats are solid or nearly solid at normal temperatures, whereas oils are liquid. Both are compounds of glycerol with fatty acids. Since the proportion of oxygen in the molecule of any oil is low, oils represent highly concentrated energy reserves; hence their particular value in seeds. Oils may be classified in four main groups: drying oils, semi-drying oils, nondrying oils, and fats.

The drying oils readily absorb oxygen on exposure to air, and dry to form a thin elastic film. These oils are valuable as solvents for pigments in paints and varnishes. Linseed oil from the flax plant (*Linum usitatissimum*), soy oil from the soybean (*Glycine max*), and safflower oil from *Carthamus tinctorius* are important examples.

The semi-drying oils also absorb oxygen, but produce only a soft film after long exposure to air. Many edible oils, illuminating oils, and those oils important in the manufacture of soaps are in this group. Cottonseed oil, sesame oil (from *Sesamum indicum*), melon-seed oil and sunflower-seed oil are all semi-drying oils. The sunflower (*Helianthus annuus*) is of particular interest as the only major crop plant that originated in what is now the United States.

The nondrying oils remain liquid at normal temperatures and do not form a film on exposure to air, because they do not react with oxygen or, at most, do so only very slowly. This group includes many of the edible and lubricating oils, olive oil, peanut oil, and castor oil.

Last, and quite unusual among the plant oils, are those that are more or less solid in cool conditions and are grouped together as plant fats. Three of the plant fats are well-known edible materials: coconut oil (from *Cocos nucifera*), palm oil (from *Elaeis guineensis*) and cacao butter (from *Theobroma cacao*).

The largest oil-producing crops of the present day grow in tropical, subtropical, or, at best, warm-temperate regions, and it may be that this fact has some significance from the standpoint of plant metabolism—a point that has not yet been fully investigated. It is of great importance, however, to the future economic development of tropical regions that they are such large suppliers of plant oils and fats.

Oil Palm

Although it is almost invidious to pick out individual oil plants for description, the oil palm, *Elaeis guineensis* (Fig. 8-4), a native of tropical Africa, deserves special mention. This palm, which grows up to 30 feet in height, bears pinnate leaves armed with spines at their bases. Its fruits are produced in a fashion rather similar to that of coconut palms, but they are actually about the size of walnuts.

Although wild oil palms have been used for centuries, they have been brought into plantation culture only within the last hundred years. Nigeria, in West Africa, is by far the largest exporter of palm oil, but the tree has also been introduced into southeast Asia and the American tropics. The oil palm provides a higher yield of oil per acre than any other oil-seed crop.

Figure 8-4. An African oil palm (*Elaeis guineensis*) growing in the Fairchild Tropical Garden, Miami, Florida.

Palm oil itself is extracted from the fleshy part of the fruit (the mesocarp), while palm-kernel oil is extracted from the kernels or seeds.

Palm oil is yellow to orange-red in color, and is more or less solid at the temperatures that prevail in so-called temperate regions of the world. Consequently, it qualifies as a plant fat. It is used in the manufacture of soap, margarine, and candles, and also as a lubricating substance in the steel and tinplate industries. It is a valuable item in the diet of West Africans, for its color is due to the presence of carotene (a source material of vitamin A). On the other hand, palm-kernel oil is thoroughly liquid even at "normal" temperatures, and is colorless or light yellow. It also has a use in the manufacture of soap and margarine.

Extra emphasis is being placed nowadays on the production of cooking oils and margarine from so-called polyunsaturated oils, which are mostly of vegetable origin, for these seem to cause less cholesterol to accumulate in blood vessels, lessening the likelihood of arteriosclerosis. An oil is said to be "saturated" when all of the carbon atoms are linked only by single valence bonds. The more double bonds there are, the more "unsaturated" the oil is. Progressive saturation of the oil, which is usually accompanied by a raising

Figure 8-5. Flowering shoot of safflower (*Carthamus tinctorius*), showing how the flower heads are enclosed in prickly bracts.

of the melting point, can be accomplished by the process of "hydrogenation." This is employed, for example, in making margarine from liquid vegetable oils. One of the most unsaturated of vegetable oils is a constituent of the mixture of oils in safflower seeds and, for this reason, the acreage alloted to the safflower, particularly in California and Arizona, is increasing every year.

The safflower (*Carthamus tinctorius*) is a member of the family Compositae (Fig. 8-5) and appears to be a native of western Asia, where about 20 other species occur. Its fruits have been found in Egyptian tombs 3500 years old, and it has been cultivated on a moderately large scale for many centuries in India, the Middle East, and East Africa. It was originally cultivated for the flower heads, from which an orange dye can be extracted. This natural pigment has now been replaced by synthetic dyes, but the oil from the seeds has become much more important.

The plant is an annual, and the one-seeded fruits, or achenes, that are produced in the heads contain between 24 and 36 per cent of their weight in oil. In addition to being edible, this oil is useful for the production of white and light-colored paints since it does not yellow with age as linseed oil (the other major oil used for this purpose) does. Safflower oil is also an important constituent of many livestock feeds, as is the seed cake that remains after the oil is expressed.

Breeding programs are in progress to increase the resistance of safflower plants to fungus diseases, insect pests and freezing temperatures. Higher oil contents (up to 50 per cent) and different oil constitutions are being sought, while the quality of the protein in the seed cake is also being improved at the same time as the bitter principles are removed. Many of these programs involve artificial hybridization with wild species that have been grown from seeds brought back to the U.S.A. from *Carthamus*-collecting expeditions to Asia.

It is to be expected that the oil plants of the world will be some of the most valuable crops of the future (see Chapter 15). Because so many of the oil plants are best grown in the tropics and subtropics, their development will be of increasing importance to the emergent nations of those zones.

9

Beverages and the Emergence
of Tropical Nations

The beverages that civilized man consumes are of two kinds: alcoholic and nonalcoholic. Both have a social function; the nonalcoholic beverages are stimulants, whereas the alcoholic ones (contrary to much popular belief) are depressants. The stimulating effects of nonalcoholic beverages come from the alkaloids that they contain and which are extracted from the source materials, along with their flavors, by hot water. These alkaloids either are caffeine or are closely related to that substance. The most highly favored alkaloid-containing beverage materials are tea, coffee, cocoa (or chocolate) and cola, and this is also the order of their consumption in the world today. Each one is a product of the tropics or the near-tropics.

Presumably, there is some biochemical significance in the fact that these taxonomically unrelated plants grow in tropical environments and produce caffeine or its close relatives, but the nature of the connection is not known. In any case, it is remarkable that different parts of unrelated plants have been adopted by isolated peoples for the same purpose — the extraction of related stimulating alkaloids: (1) theobromine, from the seeds of the cacao tree in tropical America (called cocoa in West Africa), and also from cola seeds in Africa; and (2) caffeine, from cacao and cola seeds as well as from the seeds of the coffee plant (also in Africa) and from leaves of the tea bush in Asia. Seeds from Cola nitida are chewed in Africa in order to postpone fatigue; the leaves of the coca plant (*Erythroxylon coca*), which contain cocaine, another alkaloid, serve the same function for Andean Indians.

Tea

In the case of tea, it is the leaves that provide the material for extraction by hot water. Tea made in this manner is drunk by roughly one-half the world's population, and it has an extremely long history, for it was known in ancient China, where it was first used as a medicine. Tea drinking as a social custom began in about the fifth century A.D., and from China it spread all over the world. The custom was imported to Western Europe at the end of the sixteenth or beginning of the seventeenth century, arriving after coffee-drinking had become established in favor. Even today more tea is grown in China than anywhere else, but the greatest exporting countries are India and Sri Lanka (Ceylon).

Figure 9-1. A tea bush (*Camellia sinensis*) showing the white flowers that are produced if the leafy shoots are not continuously "plucked." Grown at University of California Botanical Garden.

Figure 9-2. Tea bushes on a steep slope in a tea estate near Kandy, Sri Lanka. The pruned bushes are overtopped by small planted trees (often of the Leguminosae) whose foliage is cut and dug into the soil as a green manure.

The tea plant, as usually grown, is an evergreen shrub. It would grow into a small tree, but is normally kept as a shrub by careful pruning (Fig. 9-1). It belongs to the family Theaceae, and is usually classified as a species of the ornamental genus *Camellia*, being given the name *Camellia sinensis* (although sometimes accorded generic status on its own as *Thea sinensis*). The tea plant does not grow well on hot, humid plains or in areas where frost occurs. Consequently, the best conditions are provided by hilly country in tropical lands (Fig. 9-2), or in the subtropics at lower elevations. The rainfall must exceed 60 inches and must be well distributed throughout the year.

The plants are largely self-sterile and therefore cross-pollinating, yet they are propagated by seed. As a consequence, individual plants may vary considerably from one another because of genetical recombination. Nevertheless, it is possible to distinguish two major types, the large-leaved Indian types and the narrow-leaved Chinese types, the latter being hardier in the face of cold weather. In all probability, these two types of tea plant may have had separate origins. The Indian variety probably originated from wild plants near the source of the Irrawaddy River, in Assam or northern Burma, whereas the Chinese type may have had its origin in China itself.

On tea estates, the tea bushes are grown under partial shade, with leguminous trees being particularly favored for this purpose since their leaves can be plowed into the soil to enrich it (Fig. 9-2). In the usually hilly terrain, this building up of the soil fertility is necessary because continual erosion occurs, especially during heavy rains.

Tea leaves are produced in "flushes," and in the plant's third or fourth year of life the newly produced flush of young leaves and the stem tip are picked. For the best quality teas, only the terminal bud and the first two leaves of the young shoot are plucked; for poorer quality teas, as many as four leaves may be included. The removal of the terminal bud stimulates the development of lateral buds and a new plucking may be possible only ten days after the first one. After a number of flushes, the bush is once again pruned back to a suitable picking height. After about ten years, the whole bush may be pruned to the ground, allowing sucker shoots to produce new growth.

The treatment of the harvested leaves in factories on the tea estates varies according to whether green tea or black tea is to be produced. Green tea is made from unfermented leaves, which are steamed, rolled, dried, and then packed. Black tea, on the other hand, requires a fermentation process, during which caffeine is liberated from its chemical association with so-called tannins, and the aroma and color of tea develops. Black tea is used much more frequently in Europe and in the United States.

A prepared tea leaf contains up to five per cent caffeine, as well as 20 per cent of so-called tannins (actually quinones), which, along with pectins and dextrins, give astringency and color to the beverage. The essential oil, theol, gives the flavor and aroma. Finally, there are the nonextractable cellulose and other structural materials.

Tea from different producers and from different areas varies in the relative proportions of the constituents; as a consequence, teas must be blended before final packing for the consumer. This blending allows the idiosyncrasies of local tastes to be catered for. The blends that are most popular in the United States, for example, have much less "tannin" in them than those that are appreciated in England and Australia.

Coffee

Almost as popular as tea on the world scale is the use of coffee as a beverage. Coffee is produced from the seeds of species of *Coffea*, a genus of the Rubiaceae. There are some 50 to 60 species of *Coffea* and all are evergreen shrubs or small trees native to the rain forests of tropical and subtropical Africa. Thus, for cultivation, coffee trees require a hot, moist climate with a rainfall of up to 100 inches a year. Because they originated as undergrowth trees in the forests, they usually need to be grown in shade, at least in their early stages, and they are rather particular in their soil requirements.

Whereas tea is a crop that originated in eastern Asia and has largely stayed there in cultivation, coffee, on the other hand, originated in Africa but is now mostly grown in the New World. We shall see later that cocoa (or chocolate) is of New World origin but that most of the world's supply now comes from Africa. This is not an unusual picture among economic plants, particularly those of the tropics, but it requires a little explanation. The most cogent reason for growing economic plants in separate geographical regions from those in which they are native is that in this way they are removed from diseases and pests that have evolved along with them. This is particularly important when they are grown in large numbers in pure stands on plantations—conditions highly favorable for the spread of epidemic diseases.

The best-quality coffee is produced from *Coffea arabica*, and this species supplies the bulk of the world output. Despite its name, this small, slender-trunked tree probably originated in Ethiopia. It thrives in tropical, montane situations, and is now more frequently grown in Kenya, as well as in Brazil, Colombia, Costa Rica, and other tropical American countries. Other species can be grown in more lowland situations, but, in the quality of their product and in subtlety of flavor, they are not as good as *Coffea arabica*. However, *C. canephora*, a native of Central Africa, has become more important in recent years in providing beans for the manufacture of "instant" coffee. Its stronger flavor survives the evaporation of the coffee brew to make a better powder than that from *C. arabica*.

The flowers of *Coffea arabica* are produced in dense clusters in the axils of the leaves, and they appear in "flushes" as often as three or four times a year. The pure white blossoms (Fig. 9-3) have a beautiful and delicate scent. They open in the morning, but are faded by midday, by which time they have been pollinated by insects. The fruit is green at first, but ripens over a period of up to nine months to a red color, for which reason it is called a "cherry." When it is ripe, the deep-red outer coat of the fruit surrounds a yellowish pulp, within which there is a thin, hard inner fruit wall called the "parchment." Inside the fruit are two seeds ("beans"), which are gray-green in color and up to one-half inch in length. They are pressed together on flattened, grooved surfaces and covered with a thin seed-coat (the "silver skin").

Coffee bushes start producing fruit at about three years of age and continue producing for as many as 40 years. When ripe, the fruits are picked (by hand), washed, and pulped to remove the seeds (which are still covered with the parchment and so remain in pairs). The last remains of the pulp may be removed by fermentation in large open trays covered with water, and the seeds are next spread in the sun to dry. Subsequently, the parchment is removed by

Figure 9-3. Coffee (*Coffea arabica*) flowers and fruits (cherries). Reproduced by courtesy of the Pan-American Coffee Bureau, New York.

abrasion, causing the seeds to separate from each other, and they are then polished and packed for export. They must be roasted and ground before the beverage can be extracted, and these processes are usually left until almost the last moment before consumption. Coffees from various growing areas are usually blended together in the consuming country to assure a consistent taste that is known to be appreciated by the people of that country (Fig. 9-4). The caffeine content of roasted seeds is approximately 1 to 2 per cent of their dry weight. The roasted seeds also contain the essential oil caffeol, along with glucose, dextrins, and proteins. Decaffeinated coffee is produced by removing almost all the caffeine from green beans by various treatments with steam, acids, alkalis or organic solvents.

Domestication of coffee first took place in Arabia, to which it had been brought from the Ethiopian highlands, where it is native, in about the sixth century A.D. At first it was used as a food. For this, the powdered seeds were made into balls with butter, and these were carried on desert journeys to provide both stimulant and food. The usefulness of coffee beans in making a beverage appears to have been discovered in Arabia in the fifteenth century. The cultivation of coffee bushes did not extend into the tropics of Asia until the Dutch introduced bushes to Sri Lanka and Java at the end of the seventeenth century.

Chapter 9

In the New World, cultivation of this crop came even later. The original source of the trees in most present-day coffee plantations here was a single tree sent from Java to Amsterdam, where it was grown in the botanical garden. Seeds from this tree were sent to Surinam in 1718; this led to plantings in French Guiana and, eventually, to the establishment of the enormous Brazilian coffee industry in 1727. A descendant of the original tree in Amsterdam was sent to the Jardin des Plantes in Paris, and this provided the seed for the French introduction of coffee into the Caribbean island of Martinique in 1720. From these introductions, coffee was spread throughout the New World. Even Hawaiian and Philippine coffee trees are derived from the lonely tree in Amsterdam. This is a striking illustration of the role played by botanical gardens in the history of colonial (and later national) development in the tropics. Coffee is now produced all around the world between the tropics of Capricorn and Cancer.

At one time Sri Lanka (Ceylon) was the leading coffee-producing country in the Indian Ocean. However, a one-crop economy is very dangerous for any country, and this was made plain in the nineteenth century when, in a few years, disease swept through the island and eliminated the coffee plantations.

Figure 9-4. Coffee beans from various sources are roasted and then tasted by a "coffee taster," who blends them in appropriate proportions to produce consistent, well-appreciated flavor. Reproduced by courtesy of the Pan-American Coffee Bureau, New York.

This disease, called "leaf spot" or "coffee rust," was due to a fungus, *Hemileia vastatrix,* and its history is a fascinating one of neglect and ignorance on the part of the planters, followed by the first serious scientific investigation of the spread of a fungus plant disease by an English plant pathologist, H. Marshall Ward. The investigation, however, came too late to save the coffee industry, which was virtually extinct by the end of the century. Fortunately for Sri Lanka, however, there was another crop ready to take the place of coffee, and this was tea. Coffee rust is widespread in Africa, and in 1970 it was found in Brazil. Since it appeared more recently in Nicaragua, it seems apparent that the disease now has a foothold in the New World.

Coffee has been drunk as a beverage on a worldwide scale only in the last 300 years, beginning when small shipments were made from Arabia to western Europe at the beginning of the seventeenth century. Nevertheless, apart from its consumption in the home, the cafes of continental Europe and the coffee houses of the English-speaking countries soon became enormously important foci for social and political gatherings.

The first coffee houses were set up in Cairo at the beginning of the sixteenth century, but it was in England that their social effects have been recorded most clearly. The first coffee house in England was opened in 1650 in the university town of Oxford, and it was soon followed by others in London. These rapidly became an integral part of the daily life of the better-educated Londoner, who at nominal cost could gather with other patrons for relaxation, intellectual discussion, and refreshment. The number of coffee houses increased, and each house developed a character of its own, until every rank and profession and every kind of religious and political opinion had its own headquarters.

The best-known coffee houses were opened during the Puritan Commonwealth (1649–1659), and they provided excellent political meeting places. It was in Miles' Coffee House that the first ballot box was introduced and used. When Charles II came to power, the importance of the coffee house as a public meeting place increased. Parliament was rarely called, and there was little contact between the government and the people; the press was subject to governmental regulation, and informative books and publications were also controlled. Consequently, the coffee houses became news centers, and handwritten papers posted on coffee-house walls kept the public informed. In 1675, King Charles II tried to suppress the coffee houses, but the public outcry was so great that within 11 days the king backed down and revoked his proclamation.

Cocoa or Chocolate

Our third beverage-producing plant is the cacao tree, *Theobroma cacao,* of the Sterculiaceae. Its beans (or seeds) produce cocoa, otherwise known as chocolate. The prepared chocolate, whether in eating or drinking form, contains the alkaloids theobromine and caffeine. Chocolate is a New World contribution to man's dietary list even though the trees are now more frequently grown in the Old World than in the New.

The genus *Theobroma* is native to the forests of tropical Central and South America. The Mayas and Aztecs cultivated it, and it was encountered in 1519 by Cortéz in his conquest of present-day Mexico. The Aztec name for the beverage, *chocolatl*, was changed by the Spaniards to make it more easily pronounced by Europeans.

Theobroma seeds have apparently been collected since antiquity in South America, and *T. cacao*, the species most often cultivated today, had its origin on the lower eastern slopes of the Andes in the Upper Amazon basin, where it grows as an evergreen tree in warm, shady, humid conditions in the lower layers of the rain forests. The same conditions must be present in any area where it is to be planted nowadays, and these are usually found within ten degrees north and south of the equator. A rainfall of at least 45 inches is required. The tree is propagated from seed and also raised from cuttings.

The Mayas and the Aztecs made chocolate by pounding cacao seeds along with maize grains and then boiling the powder with water, adding capsicum peppers. The Spaniards substituted sugar and vanilla for the capsicum peppers, making an infusion of the mixture, as is done today. However, they still found it necessary to add maize flour to counteract the unpalatability resulting from the high fat content of the cacao beans.

At first, cacao beans were exported to Spain only from Central America; then, in 1525, the Spaniards planted cacao trees in Trinidad, and later established cacao-tree plantations in Venezuela, all the while restricting the export of the beans to Spain. Finally, the Spanish monopoly was broken when the Dutch settled the island of Curaçao and exported Venezuelan cacao to the rest of Europe. Thus, cocoa or chocolate became better known at the end of the sixteenth century, though it still was consumed only as a drinking chocolate, a luxury item. It was not until the early nineteenth century that C. J. van Houten in Holland developed the process currently used to remove excess fat and make drinking chocolate a much more palatable beverage. By contrast, for the making of eating chocolate, extra fat (cocoa butter) must be added and this is obtained from the defatting of the drinking chocolate. In 1876, M. D. Peter, in Switzerland, conceived the idea of adding dried milk to eating chocolate to produce "milk chocolate." Cocoa butter itself has a diminishing pharmaceutical use.

The Spaniards introduced the cacao tree into the Philippines in the seventeenth century and the Dutch carried it to Sri Lanka and Indonesia. All of these are producing areas today. In South America, the growing of cacao was confined to Venezuela by Spanish edict until the Spanish grip began to relax at

Figure 9-5. Cacao tree (*Theobroma cacao*) in Ghana, West Africa, bearing fruits directly from the trunk.

the end of the eighteenth century. Then it began to be grown in Ecuador and other countries with suitable climates.

Brazil was one of the last of the South American countries to grow plantation cacao because of its Portuguese rather than Spanish heritage. In time, however, Brazil became by far the largest exporter of cacao in the New World, and, by the end of the nineteenth century, exported more cacao than any other country in the world. After slavery was abolished in 1888, Brazilian cacao was grown by freed slaves (who had been in bondage on sugar plantations). They grew their crops on small holdings, a point of interest because this is the manner in which the crop is grown today in West Africa, currently the world's greatest producing area.

The Dutch also introduced cacao to the island of Sâo Tomé, in the Gulf of Guinea, off the west coast of Africa, which they owned from 1641 to 1844. When Sâo Tomé passed back to its original discoverers, the Portuguese, the plantations became prolific producers of cacao. From Sâo Tomé, the plant was introduced into West Africa by an indentured laborer, returning to the mainland in 1878 or 1879, and, gradually, West African countries became the world's leading producers of cacao beans.

In 1900, the Western Hemisphere produced 81 per cent of the world's cacao crop, mostly in Brazil, Ecuador, Venezuela, and Trinidad. The proportion that was produced in the Old World came largely from Sâo Tomé. By 1951, West Africa produced more than 60 per cent of the world's cacao, with the Gold Coast (now Ghana) producing 35 per cent; Nigeria, 14 per cent; and the French Cameroons, 6 per cent. Brazil's contribution dropped to only 17 per cent, even though as much cacao as ever was being exported. The reason was the greatly increased worldwide demand for chocolate, which has been met largely by West Africa.

The story of the rise of West Africa as a cacao producer is a romantic one. Until recently, the biggest chocolate manufacturers in the British Isles were family firms, and these families were Quakers. In the nineteenth century, they took exception to the manner in which indentured labor was used on the plantations on Sâo Tomé, and, when the peasant production of cacao began on the West African mainland, the manufacturers gave it their support.

Cacao flowers and the pods (fruits) that develop from them are directly attached to the trunks and main branches of the trees (Fig. 9-5), and the pods are easily harvested by cutting. They are opened by slashing the husks with a knife or by striking two pods together, and the cacao beans (the seeds) are then removed (Fig. 9-6). The seeds are then subjected to a fermentation process

Figure 9-6. Pod of cacao split open, showing contents (left) and exterior (right). The seeds have begun to germinate inside this old pod. Photograph by W. H. Hodge from Ward's Natural Science Establishment, Inc. Reproduced by permission.

that kills the embryo in each seed, releasing enzymes that produce the "pre-cursors" of chocolate flavor (which are finally brought out only much later, when the beans are roasted at a factory). During fermentation, the cotyledons in the seed change to a rich purple-brown color, resembling that of chocolate itself. The beans are then dried. Generally, the fermented beans are exported to Europe and the U.S., where the process of chocolate manufacture is completed.

After World War II there was a great boom in world cacao prices, and the increased wealth that this brought to the cacao-producing countries has had a tremendous effect on their social and political status. In Ghana, for instance, where the marketing of cacao is done by the government, the difference between the fixed price paid to the farmers and that which is received from overseas buyers has been used to build roads, schools, and hospitals. Undoubtedly, the relative wealth of this country, the former Gold Coast colony, derived from cacao, was one factor that enabled it to achieve independence from Great Britain (in 1957) ahead of its neighbors.

Ghana's dependence on a single crop is not without serious dangers, however. The greatest of these is the possibility that Swollen Shoot disease will decimate the cacao-growing industry (Fig. 9-7). This disease occurs naturally in native forest trees of three closely related families: the Sterculiaceae (to which the cacao tree also belongs), the Bombacaceae, and the Tiliaceae. The disease is caused by a virus, but it does little harm to the native trees, which, in the course of time, have become relatively tolerant of its presence (probably by the selection of resistant varieties). The cacao tree, on the other hand, being a native of South America, where the virus does not occur, has never been selected for resistance to it, and, when infected, it rapidly develops the extreme symptoms of the disease (swollen shoots, mottled and falling leaves, declining yield of fruit, and, ultimately death).

This example of a tropical crop plant meeting and suffering from a disease that is not present in its native land, after transportation to another part of the world, is an interesting reversal of the situation seen more frequently (and exemplified by Pará rubber described in Chapter 11) in which a crop plant removed from its area of origin gives better yields by escaping from the diseases and pests that have evolved along with it.

Swollen Shoot disease was first noticed in 1936, and for some time was attributed to a nutrient deficiency in the soil. It began to sweep through the cacao-growing areas of West Africa thereafter, and has only been slowed down by a vigorously applied program of cutting out obviously diseased trees. The virus is carried by sap-sucking mealy bugs from the native host plants to the cacao trees growing alongside them in the forests, and is similarly carried between cacao trees. The mealy bugs are protected from attack, as they feed on the twigs of the trees, by "cartons" built over them by ants that tend them (and "milk" them of much of the plant juices that the bugs suck from the tree).

Because of the "cartons," it has proved difficult to combat the mealy bugs with insecticidal sprays, although there has been some success in eliminating the ants. On the other hand, attempts to find and breed from resistant races of cacao trees have also been only partly successful, and there is a real danger that cacao in West Africa could suffer the same fate as coffee in Sri Lanka.

In Ghana, the industrialization and diversification of agriculture, following the building of a large dam on the Volta River, may reduce the danger of dependence on a single major export item. Nevertheless, the wider problem

Figure 9-7. Cacao trees (*Theobroma cacao*) dying from "Swollen Shoot" disease in West Africa. From D. H. Urquhart, *Cocoa*, 2nd ed. New York: John Wiley & Sons, Inc., 1961. Reproduced by permission of Cadbury Bros. Ltd., Bournville, England.

remains; it is only too typical of tropical countries that they are dependent for their economic well-being on individual export crops produced on a plantation scale. Failure of such crops can produce political and social troubles of no lesser magnitude than the advantages that come to the same countries in boom times.

10

Fermentation

Yeast

The histories of baking and brewing have much in common because yeast is utilized in both. In baking, the primary function of this one-celled fungus (Fig. 10-1) is the production of carbon dioxide to leaven the dough. In brewing, both carbon dioxide and ethyl alcohol are desirable products. In the latter process, growth of the yeast in the sugary liquid must take place under anaerobic (oxygen-poor) conditions.

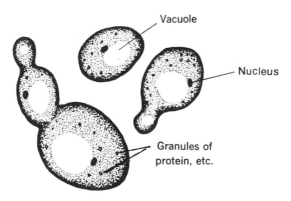

Figure 10-1. Yeast. Single-celled plants in various stages of division by budding ($\times$ 3,000).

Although alcoholic fermentations were utilized by prehistoric man, in most cases wild yeasts were employed without the users being aware of their existence, for they are microscopic and their biological nature was not appreciated until relatively recently. The Polynesians, however, who have used yeast since early times for breaking down the starch in ground seeds, appear to have been exceptional in their deliberate use and propagation of the fungus.

Since the cells of yeast (see Fig. 10-1) are too small to be seen with the naked eye, it was not until Antoni van Leeuwenhoek invented fine simple microscopes that they were discovered. He described yeast cells in 1680, but failed to recognize their connection with alcoholic fermentation. In 1803, Thénard and, later, several other investigators claimed that there was a connection, but this was disputed by von Liebig in 1840, and the controversy raged until 1859. In that year Louis Pasteur demonstrated positively that yeast is a living organism capable of growth and reproduction as well as causing fermentation of sugars with the production of alcohol. However, full details of the life cycle of a yeast were not worked out until 1943.

Alcoholic Fermentation

Throughout the world, mildly alcoholic drinks have been made from almost every kind of sugar- or starch-containing plant material. Starches and other polysaccharides need to be broken down to fermentable sugars before alcoholic fermentation can occur, and the necessary enzymes may be provided by some external source, such as human saliva in the manufacture of *chicha* (corn beer) in Andean regions, or by the yeast itself. Mead, a favorite drink in the Middle Ages, was made by fermenting a mixture of honey and water. Sake is made in Japan by fermenting rice, and pulque in Mexico is the fermented sap of various agaves.

Present-day beers and ales are made by fermenting cereal grains in water. The starch is hydrolyzed to fermentable maltose and glucose by enzymes (diastase) produced during the germination of part of the grain and the sugars are then acted on by the yeast. The alcohol content of beers and ales ranges from three to ten per cent. Wines are the fermented juice of grapes and other fruit, and contain as much as 14 per cent alcohol. A higher alcohol content cannot usually be produced (except by addition of alcohol from another source), partly because, above this concentration, the yeasts are killed by the alcohol itself. Higher concentrations of alcohol are produced by distillation, and, of the liquors made in this manner, whiskey is derived from fermented grain, brandy from wine, and rum from sugar cane products.

Brewing

The commonest source of beer in temperate regions is malt (germinated barley), but usually other cereal grains (rice and maize, in particular) are added to the germinated barley. The characteristic bitter flavor of beer is produced by boiling the aqueous extract of the malt and grain (the wort) with the flower buds of the hop plant, although other herbs have been used in the past. The fermentation itself takes place under cool conditions after brewers' yeast (*Saccharomyces cerevisiae*) has been added to the wort. Alcohol, flavoring substances, and carbon dioxide are produced by the action of the yeast, which is ultimately removed by settling and filtration. In most commercial breweries, further carbonation is provided before the beer is bottled or canned.

Wine-Making

Wine-making, though in some ways a less complicated process, has at least as great an antiquity as brewing. Wine grapes probably originated in southwest Asia and were in cultivation in pre-Christian times. Grapes are the fruits of woody, tendrilled vines of the genus *Vitis* (Vitaceae), the cultivated species in Europe being *V. vinifera* (Fig. 10-2). Vines brought to Europe from Asia hybridized with the native European grapevines to produce, with further selection, the varieties used in contemporary wine production. Although the process of hybridization was repeated with native American vines centuries later when the colonists carried grape cultivation to the New World, grape growing for wine and for raisin manufacture in California (the state with by far the largest grape acreage in the U.S.) depends upon introduced European stocks.

Nevertheless, in a most unusual way, American stocks were the salvation of the European wine industry following the disastrous invasion of the vineyards of France, Madeira, and the Canary Islands by scale insects known as phylloxera (*Dactylasphaera vitifoliae*) in 1863. The insects, accidentally introduced from America, attacked and destroyed the roots of 2,500,000 acres of French vines. Their ravages were ended only by the importation of phylloxera-resistant rootstocks (such as those of *Vitis rupestris*) from the eastern United States, upon which the European vines were then grafted.

Wine-making involves the fermentation of the sugars in the juice (the "must") after it has been expressed from the grapes and has been given time to settle. Wine yeast, *Saccharomyces ellipsoideus*, is used and, in fact, is usually present naturally as part of the "bloom" on the outside of the grape (see Fig. 10-2).

The chemical composition of grapes of the same variety varies when they are grown under different climatic and soil conditions, influencing the characteristics of the wine. In this, we have part of the basis for distinguishing on a quality basis between the products of different vineyards and also the variation between "vintage" and poorer years.

The distinction between red and white wines depends on the presence or absence of anthocyanin pigments in the skins of the grapes (the pomace) and also upon whether or not these skins are included with the must during the

Figure 10-2. Portion of vine with grapes of the Cabernet Sauvignon variety, the principal source of fine red wines in the Bordeaux region of France. Note the "bloom" on the grapes. Photograph courtesy of Prof. H. P. Olmo, University of California, Davis.

initial stages of fermentation. "Aging" of the wine in wooden casks usually follows its manufacture and this involves slow chemical changes that improve the flavor and bouquet.

Sweet wines may contain as much as 18 per cent sugar; dry wines may have less than 0.2 per cent. In sweet wines, fermentation may be stopped at an early stage by the addition of alcohol. In dry wines, it is allowed to go on until almost all the sugar is used up. Sparkling wines (such as champagne) are given their carbonation by the addition of sugar to a table wine followed by renewed fermentation in a tightly closed container so that the carbon dioxide that is formed cannot escape. Dessert wines are "fortified" by the addition of extra alcohol derived from wine distillation.

In countries with cool, moist climates, where grapes will not ripen, wine substitutes may be made from other fruits. Apples, for example, provide a hard cider that is well regarded in the British Isles, although beer and distilled spirits are more frequently consumed in these islands. Beer, at least, was particularly valuable in earlier days when water supplies were contaminated and the diet was unbalanced. Boiling in the preparation of beer effectively sterilized the drink, and the yeasts added vitamins, particularly riboflavin (vitamin B_2), to a diet in which they were usually lacking.

Production of Liquors by Distillation

If a concentration of alcohol much beyond 14 per cent is required, it can be produced from the products of fermentation only by distillation, a process where concentration depends on the much lower boiling point of alcohol in comparison with that of water. Because the fermented mash contains "impurities" with boiling points comparable to that of alcohol, these are carried over into the distillate to give the appropriate flavor and color. The liquor is then aged and given extra flavor with essences or fruits. Most liquors contain 40 to 50 per cent alcohol.

Whiskies, gin and vodka are distilled from fermented cereal grain mash; brandy is distilled wine; rum comes from fermented and distilled molasses; tequila is from fermented agave sap.

Whereas the production of beers and wines involves only the supervision and control of a process that also occurs naturally, the development of the production of liquors by distillation depended upon human ingenuity. Nevertheless, it seems that the ancients in China, Arabia, and Egypt had developed appropriate techniques between 2,000 and 3,000 years ago; however, it was not until Robert Stein invented the patent still in 1826 that the full range of modern spirits, liquors, and liqueurs was produced.

Other Aspects of Fermentation

This is not the place to discuss in detail the tremendous influence on human history which may be attributed to alcoholic beverages, their availability and prohibition, and the taxes that, inevitably, have been levied upon them. Certainly in the modern world their influence has been as great as that of any other plant product that can be named. Besides being used in beverages, alcohols have many commercial uses. Ethyl alcohol is used as a fuel, solvent, and raw material in a variety of industrial processes, and has many medicinal and surgical applications. Recently, Brazil has made a significant reduction in the use of gasoline for automobile fuel, substituting for it ethyl alcohol, which is made on a large scale from the carbohydrates present in sugar cane and cassava (manioc, *Manihot esculenta*).

Several commercially important chemicals are now manufactured by controlled processes of fermentation involving microorganisms other than yeast. Acetone and butyl alcohol are both products of the fermentation of corn mash by the bacterium *Clostridium acetobutylicum*. In the manufacture of vinegar, two separate fermentations are involved. Ethyl alcohol is produced in the form of wine or hard cider, or from barley malt; it is then converted to acetic acid by species of *Acetobacter* growing in aerated conditions. Citric acid, much used in the preparation of soft drinks, is produced by the action of the fungus *Aspergillus niger* upon sugar, and this process has almost completely replaced its commercial derivation from lemons. Soy sauce is produced from a mixture of soya beans, wheat flour, and salt, fermented with the fungus *Aspergillus oryzae*, an ancient process which has lasted till the present day. Enzymatic fermentations are also involved in the production of tea, coffee, and cocoa (as was noted in Chapter 9) although, of course, the beverages produced from them contain no alcohol. The production of such diverse materials as silage, sauerkraut, yogurt, and cheese involve the activities of bacteria generally included in the genus *Lactobacillus,* the most important fermentative product of which is lactic acid. Finally, the very modern antibiotics, of which penicillin was the forerunner, are the products of the metabolism of fungi and bacteria (see Chapter 13). In many ways it seems that through fermentations of various sorts, lower plants are likely to play an increasing part in human affairs in the future.

11

The Story
of Rubber

One of the most dramatic events in the twentieth-century history of economic plant materials has been the spectacular rise of rubber to a position of indispensability. Included in this drama is the history of the Pará rubber tree (*Hevea brasiliensis*), which involves stories of exploration, smuggling, and empire-building.

Chemically, rubber is an amorphous hydrocarbon belonging to the group known as polyterpenes (actually "*cis*-polyisoprene"), a name that reminds us of the essential oils, some of which are terpenes. Like the essential oils, rubber is produced in specialized cells as a product of the metabolism of carbohydrates. In these cells, the rubber forms a constituent of latex, a white or yellow, slightly viscous fluid that is usually seen when it exudes from the cut surface of a stem, leaf, or root to seal off a wound. The rubber in latex occurs as microscopic particles floating in water as a colloidal solution along with starch, oil globules, and other materials. Only certain families of plants produce latex, and, among these, only some — all of them dicotyledons — produce a latex that contains rubber.

The specialized cells that carry latex are either latex tubes or latex vessels, depending on the plant family involved. Each kind of container extends throughout the plant. A latex tube is derived from a single cell that grows and branches in the embryo plant, keeping pace with the growth of the plant itself. Although the tube may develop many nuclei, it never develops any cross walls, and remains a single cell ramifying throughout the plant. On the other hand, a latex vessel is produced in much the same way as a xylem vessel, by the breakdown of the end walls between a number of longitudinally opposed cells.

Rubber is produced as a tropical crop with only a few exceptions. It was known to primitive tropical peoples, particularly in the New World, but it does not appear to have been fully appreciated by the world at large until the nineteenth century. Consequently, the demand for this substance is a relatively recent one, and of course depends on the rise to a dominant position in our lives of automobiles, airplanes, and electrical apparatus. Production of rubber has more than quadrupled in the last 50 years, and now more than 2,000,000 tons of natural rubber are produced every year, despite the discovery and production of synthetic substitutes.

The most important source of rubber at the present day is the Pará rubber tree, *Hevea brasiliensis* (of the family Euphorbiaceae). Despite the fact that it is a native of the tropical rain forests of Amazonia, very little rubber now comes from the wild and semi-cultivated trees of that region. At least 92 per cent of the rubber produced today comes from southeast Asia, particularly Malaya and Indonesia, with some from Central and West Africa. Thus, rubber provides us with another example of the intercontinental transplantation of a crop plant to a position of great importance in the region into which it has immigrated, while it remains relatively unimportant in its native region.

Hevea brasiliensis is a tree growing to about 60 feet in height, with a trunk up to six feet in girth. Its compound leaves bear three leaflets, and its small, green, sweetly scented flowers are arranged in inflorescences that contain pistillate flowers in the upper part and staminate flowers below. The fruits are three-lobed, and each lobe contains a single seed (Fig. 11-1). In their endosperm, the seeds (which look rather like castor beans) contain an oil that resembles linseed oil, as well as a cyanide-producing glycoside.

Rubber was first encountered by Europeans in Mexico, where Cortéz saw the natives playing ball games with balls made of rubber. The rubber may have been produced from the tree *Castilla elastica* (a member of the fig family, the Moraceae). In addition, rubber from *Hevea* has been used since prehistoric times by Amazonian Indians to make watertight containers, balls, and other articles. The Spanish conquistadors took over its use for waterproofing their hats and clothes by smearing them with the latex from the tree.

Prepared rubber was shipped to Europe as a curiosity but uses were not found for it immediately. It was not until 1770 that Joseph Priestley in England discovered its ability to erase pencil marks on paper; it was this property that led to its being called rubber. Previously it had been known by a corruption of the Indian name, which was rendered in European writings as "caoutchouc."

In 1823, a Scot named MacIntosh showed that rubber could be dissolved in naphtha. This means that cloth can be waterproofed, even when fresh latex is not available, by impregnating the material with the rubber solution and allowing the solvent to evaporate, leaving rubber particles in the tissues of the cloth. As a result of this discovery, raincoats are known to this day in Britain as "mackintoshes."

Figure 11-1. Leaves and fruits of the Pará rubber tree (*Hevea brasiliensis*).

However, the most significant date is 1839, the year in which Goodyear in the U.S. invented vulcanization. Normally, rubber becomes soft with heat and brittle with cold. He found that chemical combination with sulfur under heat (150° C) and pressure cures both troubles and gives the rubber toughness and resistance to wear. This discovery permitted the later use of rubber on a tremendous scale in the manufacture of automobile and bicycle tires, which in turn made it a vital munition in war. The invasion of southeast Asia by the Japanese in World War II was impelled in part by their need for rubber and by their desire to deny it to the Allies.

At first, rubber was collected by cutting down the wild trees of *Hevea brasiliensis* in the Amazonian rain forests. As the value of rubber increased in the nineteenth century, the Brazilian government placed a ban on the export of seeds. Nevertheless, seeds were collected there in 1873 by a Englishman named Farris, and they were sent to the Royal Botanic Gardens at Kew, in London. The seeds were germinated there because, as in so many tropical plants, they retain their viability for only a short time, shorter than the length of the voyage that would have been needed to take them all the way to the southeast Asian tropics, where it had been decided that a new industry should be started. The plants that resulted from Farris's collection were finally shipped to another Royal Botanic Garden at Calcutta, India, but failed to thrive there and were lost.

Another attempt to collect *Hevea* seeds was made by Henry Wickham (later knighted) in 1875. Wickham was commissioned by the British government to collect rubber tree seeds, which he did along the banks of the Amazon. He was able to charter a small ship, and he loaded its decks with baskets of the seeds labeled "delicate specimens for Queen Victoria's gardens at Kew." Accounts vary on whether or not the Brazilian customs authorities knew what they were letting through. Wickham reached London with 70,000 seeds on June 14, 1876. It is reported that he hired a train and then a cab and drove with all speed to Kew, calling on Sir Joseph Hooker, Director of the Gardens, late that night. Next morning, greenhouses were emptied of other plants and the rubber tree seeds were all sown and kept under hot, humid conditions. Less than 3,000 of them germinated but a few months later about 1,900 young plants were old enough to be sent by ship to Sri Lanka as deck cargo in 38 miniature greenhouses. A gardener looked after them on the voyage, and about 1700 seedlings were landed in Sri Lanka in growing condition. From these plants and others sent to Singapore, the vast rubber industries of Sri Lanka, Malaya, and Indonesia were developed. The total cost of the introduction of the young plants to southeast Asia was less than £1500 (about $6,000 at that time). By 1968, the plantations started from them and their descendants were producing about two million tons of rubber a year.

Even though the rubber trees were introduced to southeast Asia before the end of the nineteenth century, they did not begin immediately to play an important role in the economy of that area. At this time, tin mining and coffee growing were the major economic supports of the countries, and it took a sustained propaganda effort by Sir Henry Ridley, Director of the Royal Botanic Gardens at Singapore, to convince the estate owners there that they should take up rubber production. He also devised the tapping method of obtaining the latex from trees without destroying them.

Successful rubber plantations under American direction have been established in Liberia, in West Africa. On the other hand, numerous attempts to establish plantations in Brazil, the home of rubber, have failed for a variety of reasons, including the presence of indigenous diseases from which the plantations in southeast Asia and West Africa have been free. Worst of these diseases is the leaf blight caused by a fungus, *Dothidella ulei*.

The latex is obtained from rubber trees by tapping, beginning when the tree is six years old. As Fig. 11-2 shows, the latex vessels are borne in concentric rings, alternating with rings of phloem tissues. Consequently, tapping consists of making an incision in the bark shallow enough not to damage the cambium that produces the new rings of latex vessels and phloem, but sufficiently deep

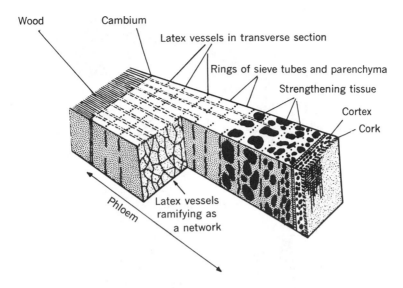

Wood

Cambium

Latex vessels in transverse section

Rings of sieve tubes and parenchyma

Strengthening tissue

Cortex

Cork

Phloem

Latex vessels
ramifying as
a network

Figure 11-2. Diagram of outer tissues of Pará rubber tree (*Hevea brasiliensis*) showing the arrangement of rows of latex vessels in the phloem.

to allow the latex in the more peripheral rings to exude. First a vertical incision is made, and then a spiral cut is made one-third to halfway around the tree (Fig. 11-3); alternatively, a "V" cut is made. The latex flows down and is collected in a cup. The flow begins in the morning and ceases by midday. As a consequence, the cut surfaces must be renewed each morning, or at least on alternate mornings, and this may be continued for several months.

The latex is conveyed to the factory and coagulated by the addition of acetic acid or formic acid, producing a white, spongy mass, which is then pressed between rollers and dried, producing sheets of crepe rubber. Often the sheets are treated further by being smoked in smoke houses. Here the material is heated to about 45° C and exposed to the vapors from burning wood. These contain "pyroligneous acids" which cause a darkening and induction of translucence in the rubber, producing the so-called "smoke-sheet." Most of the rubber that is exported to Europe and the U.S. is of this form, and it is, of course, processed further there.

For some purposes it is more expedient to export the latex itself; in this case, it is centrifuged to concentrate it and an anticoagulant, usually aqueous ammonia (NH_4OH), is added. Then the latex can be shipped in liquid form to the receiving country.

These modern methods of treating the latex to produce rubber are in striking contrast to the primitive methods still employed by the Indians in Amazonia. There, the latex from wild or semi-wild trees is collected, and, once again,

Figure 11-3. Sri Lankan rubber tapper at work in the early morning on a tree of Pará rubber (*Hevea brasiliensis*). Photograph courtesy of Prof. J. W. Purseglove, Imperial College of Tropical Agriculture, Trinidad.

pyroligneous acid from burning wood is used in its treatment. Latex is poured onto a paddle, which is held in the smoke over a burning fire. The pyroligneous acid in the smoke causes the latex to coagulate, whereupon more latex is poured on the paddle (and its existing load), which continues to be rotated until it produces a smoked ball that may weigh as much as 200 pounds. These balls are then loaded onto river craft and shipped down the Amazon River to be exported.

The proportion of the world's rubber produced by the smoked-ball method is small at the present time. This was not always the case, however, and at the end of the nineteenth century the demand for rubber was so great that the Amazonian forests witnessed the equivalent of a gold rush. The price of rubber soared to over three dollars a pound, and it was in such circumstances as these, around 1910, that the city of Manaus on the Rio Negro, a tributary of the Amazon, flourished. In the midst of the sweltering Amazon forest, this city boasted opera houses, luxurious hotels, and wild living. Another milder boom occurred during the Second World War. In contrast to these "booms," however, there were disastrous "busts" when the price of rubber fell as low as two cents a pound.

Substitute Rubber Sources

As with most crops that are the products of tropical regions, the vulnerability of their supply to temperate civilizations is pointed up most clearly in wartime. In both world wars, the shortage of rubber led European and American scientists to search for alternatives. In addition to the organization of protracted searches through the native floras of temperate regions to find alternative latex-producing plants, chemists were put to work to produce a synthetic rubber.

The most famous of the substitute rubber plants used in World War II was guayule (*Parthenium argentatum*), a native of the southwestern United States and Mexico, much worked on in California. This plant is a small shrub belonging to the Compositae, and it grows in desert regions. Another member of the same family, the Russian dandelion (*Taraxacum kok-saghyz*), was put to similar use in the Soviet Union. In both cases it is necessary to sacrifice the plant in the extraction of the latex, for this is taken from the roots; and in neither case did it prove profitable to continue the extraction of rubber after the return to availability of the tropical sources of Pará rubber. Continuous progress has been maintained in the production of synthetic rubber, which at first was not only expensive to produce but less durable than natural rubber. Synthetic rubbers have been greatly improved in quality, and now most automobile tires consist of blends of natural and synthetic rubber. However, petrochemicals are rapidly becoming more expensive and may be expected to become scarcer as petroleum reserves in the world grow smaller, so there has been a consequent resurgence of interest in guayule as a source of natural rubber, along with continued production from *Hevea*.

Balatas

Balatas are also products of coagulated latex, in this case derived from various trees belonging to the family Sapotaceae, which are native to tropical countries. The balatas differ from rubber in that, although they yield to pressure, they are not flexible. Consequently, they can be molded into a particular shape in which they will stay. Among the balatas of economic importance are gutta percha (from *Palaquium gutta* in Malaya) and chewing gum. As the reader can well imagine, it would be most unfortunate if chewing gum had the elasticity of rubber.

The Story of Rubber

Originally, chewing gum was made from the latex known as chicle, most of which is obtained from the bark of the sapodilla tree, *Manilkara achras,* a native of tropical America (where its fruits are relished). According to John Purseglove, chicle was chewed by the Aztecs. However, the demand for chewing gum has grown to such an extent that it is now no longer possible for one species of wild tree (or its cultivated representatives) to supply all needs, and other members of the Sapotaceae, as well as representatives of other families (for example, the Moraceae and the Euphorbiaceae), may be called upon. In all probability, synthetic plastics will ultimately take the place of "natural" chewing gum.

12

The Contribution
of Trees

It is nearly impossible to do more than outline the ways in which forest trees and their products have been of use to man. Even though we are entering an age in which steel and plastics may seem to be outdating the use of wood, it is probable that new uses for wood and wood products are at least keeping pace with the loss of the old ones. Indeed, no material is more intimately connected with the growth and survival of our contemporary civilization than a wood product, paper. Yet as more people use (and waste) paper for more purposes every year, the outlook for the forests of the world is far from rosy. Even when the wood is not used for productive purposes, the forests are disappearing, chiefly being cleared for agricultural purposes. Almost all of the tropical rain forests will probably disappear within the next century, yet it has been estimated that the economic possibilities of more than 90 per cent of the plant species in them remain unknown. Even where the forests are preserved, the most valuable timber trees have often been removed.

Nevertheless, deforestation is no new phenomenon. Archaeologists have used the evidence of the clearing of forest land in western Europe for agriculture to mark the commencement of the Neolithic (New Stone) Age in that region. Nor, in fact, is conservation new. In England, even Bronze Age man practiced a "coppice" system of forest management, in which straight poles of hazel are produced by cutting these small trees almost to soil level and then letting them sprout and grow again for up to 20 years. But when European man came to the New World, he repeated European practices of forest destruction; first to go in New England were tall trees for the masts of ships, and then timber for building purposes; finally, firewood needs were satisfied from the remains, and agricultural operations prevented the regeneration of the forests until relatively recently.

The wood that man uses is both supporting and conducting tissue for the trees that supply it. The details of its structure may be seen in any textbook on biology or botany, so most of our attention will be given to the differences to be seen between the two major kinds of wood. Figure 12-2 shows the essential constituents of a tree trunk as they appear in transverse section as well as in radial and tangential views. The cell walls of the wood tissue consist largely of cellulose together with deposits of the complex of hemicelluloses known as lignin.

In a mature tree, the wood may be divided into (1) the sapwood, the outermost parts most recently differentiated from cells produced by division in the cambium, and (2) the heartwood, the crushed, older, and, therefore, central portion of the wood (Fig. 12-1). The sapwood, which serves a conducting function for water and dissolved materials, is often less valuable for timber than the heartwood, which is drier and therefore less liable to warp or crack. The heart-

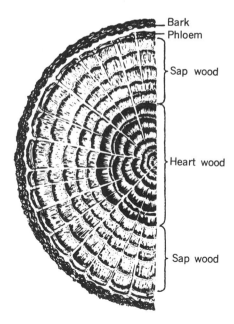

Figure 12-1. Diagram of distribution of tissues in a transverse section of a tree trunk. From E. W. Sinnott and K. S. Wilson, *Botany: Principles and Problems*, 5th ed. New York: McGraw-Hill Book Co., Inc., 1955. Reproduced by permission.

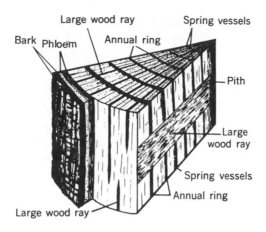

Large wood ray   Spring vessels
Bark Phloem   Annual ring

Pith

Large
wood ray

Spring vessels

Annual ring

Large wood ray

Figure 12-2. Diagram of a block of the trunk of a broad-leaved hardwood tree cut to show the arrangement of the tissues. From E. W. Sinnott and K. S. Wilson, *Botany: Principles and Problems*, 5th ed. New York: McGraw-Hill Book Co., Inc., 1955. Reproduced by permission.

wood may also be impregnated with tannins and other waste products of metabolism, which have a preservative action and give it a darker color.

With this general structure in mind, we can distinguish between "hardwoods" and "softwoods." The former are derived from trees that are dicotyledonous flowering plants, while the latter come from coniferous trees. Generally speaking, the names are truly indicative of a difference in hardness of the wood, but there is great variation between the various species of each group, and there is also considerable overlap. The softwoods contain tracheids, fibers, and parenchyma cells, but almost all hardwoods contain vessels as well (Fig. 12-2).

The greater diameter of vessels compared with tracheids, and their tendency to be produced in different proportions in spring, summer, and fall in characteristic fashion in different species, results in strikingly different "grain" patterns in the woods. When this is added to the variation in color, durability, toughness, bending strength, workability, and even odor, it is clear that man has been provided from the very commencement of his utilization of wood with the necessity of choosing the most suitable kinds for his various purposes. The influence that this necessity of choice must have had on his technological and esthetic development is incalculable but surely enormous. Whether it be in the selection of a suitable wood for the manufacture of a club, a digging stick, a bridge, a crude or elegant item of furniture, or an abstract sculpture, the choice has had to be made, and success or failure in making it has certainly been a selective factor in man's social evolution.

Wood has not been available equally to all men. A good atlas will show in general fashion the distribution of forests in the world. The softwoods (conifers) tend to be characteristic of those areas with the colder climates, although the mild Pacific Northwest harbors the most luxuriant coniferous forest growth in North America (Fig. 12-3), whereas the hardwoods are typical of restricted areas in temperate regions, and reach their greatest development in the well-watered, continuously warm equatorial "rain forests" (Fig. 12-4).

The nature and availability of forest trees have played their parts directly and indirectly in determining man's way of life in different regions of the world. Because they lacked forest trees, Eskimos and Bushmen could never push their civilizations to the technological limits reached by their most fortunate colleagues in the family of man.

Figure 12-3. Douglas firs (*Pseudotsuga menziesii*) forming a valuable coniferous forest stand in Oregon.

Figure 12-4.   Broad-leaved hardwood tropical forest at Barro Colorado Island, Panama Canal Zone.

At the present day, softwoods are particularly favored in temperate regions for building materials such as planks, plywood, and boards made from compressed sawdust. Temperate hardwoods are utilized for furniture and implements; tropical hardwoods have specialized uses in furniture and decoration (for example, mahogany), and they also provide building materials in the regions where they are grown.

Charcoal

Although wood has been used for fuel by man just as long as he has had control over fire, when a smokeless, flameless fire is required, charcoal has the advantage, and its use antedates history. Charcoal is made by covering a heap of cut hardwood with sod, earth, or leaves so that only a minimum amount of air can enter. The pile is then ignited at the bottom and burned slowly for many days (Fig. 12-5). The charcoal that is produced is a mixture of carbon and mineral ash. In addition to being burned as a fuel, it is used in the smelting of metals, in the purification of sugars, for the adsorption of gases and for making explosives (and the fuses for them). In the Middle Ages, the forests of southern England were decimated not only through the cutting of the oak trees to provide timber for building the ships of the British Navy (see Chapter 3) but also through the production of charcoal for the smelting of the local iron ore, from which their cannons were cast.

Figure 12-5. Charcoal making from broad-leaved hardwood trees in the tropical forest, Trinidad, West Indies.

Wood Distillation

By the eighteenth century, it was discovered that the vapors given off during the production of charcoal from hardwoods contained valuable chemicals and, if the process were carried on in kilns for the destructive distillation of wood, some of the vapors could be condensed as "pyroligneous acid." In addition, gases such as methane and hydrogen, and tar, methyl alcohol (wood alcohol), acetone, and acetic acid were produced in this manner, although these are now manufactured more economically by other means.

The distillation of softwoods is devoted to a different end. The sapwood and inner bark of pine trees contain "resin canals" in which pitch, a mixture of resins (terpenes) and essential oils, is found. Pitch can be obtained by tapping trees (chipping into the bark and outer wood). It has been used since pre-Christian times for caulking the seams of wooden boats and ships, leading to the name "naval stores" for the pitch industry. Distillation of pitch produces turpentine, although this may also be obtained by distilling the wood itself (using, for example, stumps left behind after lumbering). Turpentine has been in great demand as a paint thinner, but, as is usual in history, the natural product is now being replaced by cheaper synthetic substitutes. Rosin, the residue left when pitch evaporates, is also used in the paint industry and, in very specialized fashions, for the treatment of musicians' bows and to provide a foothold on the canvas of boxing rings.

Hydrolysis and Fermentation

Since wood is basically composed of cellulose, which is itself built up from glucose units, wood forms a reservoir from which sugars and sugar derivatives can be produced in quantity by hydrolysis (usually of sawdust or chips by steam containing dilute sulfuric acid, or by enzyme action). The glucose solution that results may be either concentrated for direct use or fermented to produce ethyl alcohol. Up to 65 gallons of alcohol can be produced from every ton of wood.

Pulp and Paper

Whereas sawdust is of use in the production of the wood-conversion products already referred to, wood pulp, made by a combined shredding and chemical treatment, is needed for other synthetic purposes. The loose fibers in wood pulp may be felted into paper or treated with more chemicals to produce rayon or plastics.

At first, paper was not made from wood. The earliest materials of plant origin on which writing could be practiced were prepared at least 2,000 years before Christ, in Ancient Egypt, by gumming together superimposed strips of the pith of the papyrus plant, *Cyperus papyrus*, of the Cyperaceae. This aquatic plant (from which the word "paper" derives) is still commonly grown in warmer regions of the world as a decorative plant (Fig. 12-6). In tropical Asia and Egypt, books were also made from strips of flattened and dried palm leaves (Fig. 12-7) before there was paper, while in China, "rice paper" was made by

Figure 12-6. *Cyperus papyrus.* Papyrus was made by beating out the pith of the stems.

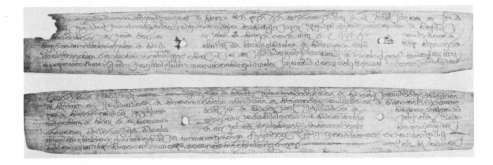

Figure 12-7. Two leaves from a palm-leaf book made in Sri Lanka. In the book, the leaves are joined by threads looped through each of the two holes.

beating out the pith of the shrub *Tetrapanax papyriferum*, of the family Araliaceae (Fig. 12-8).

True paper production is a Chinese invention, apparently made during the second century A.D. In these early times, paper was prepared by pounding rags, bark, hemp, and other fibrous materials into a pulp in water, and then placing a mold made of bamboo strips under the pulp suspended in the water. As the water drained away, the mold was shaken, causing the fibers to interlock. The mold and its contents were then placed in the sun to dry, producing a sheet of a rather porous paper (suitable, however, for painting with a brush).

The Chinese sold paper to merchants who visited their country, but kept the secret of its manufacture in the East until Arab soldiers captured Chinese paper-makers at Samarkand about 750 A.D. As Arab conquest spread across North Africa, the art of paper-making was carried with it, and, in the twelfth and thirteenth centuries, it reached Spain and Italy. A European contribution to the art, made necessary by the use of quill pens, was the coating of paper so that the ink would not spread. This was achieved by filling the pores with white lead, plaster of Paris, or other materials mixed with water.

Whereas linen and cotton rags had provided the major part of the fibers used in ancient paper-making, with the increased demand that resulted from the spread of literacy, the invention of printing, and the utilization of paper for other purposes such as wrapping, substitute sources were needed. The apparently limitless forests suggested an answer, provided that the cellulose in the wood could be separated from undesirable accompanying chemicals, notably lignin. In 1840, Friedrich Keller, a German, was the first to produce a usable paper from a mixture of wood pulp and rags, and in the next 60 years the demand for and production of paper doubled and redoubled.

The enormous growth of the paper industry has continued in the twentieth century, and has brought a grave threat to the future of the forests of North

America, where, in the U.S. alone, 25,000,000 tons of paper and paperboard are made each year. Even with energetic reforestation programs in Canada and the north-central, northwestern, and southern United States (the largest areas of pulp-producing pine trees) there is still some danger that supplies will be exhausted, since each tree requires 15 to 30 years to grow to an appropriate size for pulping. However, the threat has stimulated some positive programs, such as the creation of National Forests, to conserve forest resources. Repulping of paper and the use of alternative materials such as esparto grass (*Stipa tenacissima* — a large, tussock grass from North Africa, now particularly grown in

Figure 12-8.   Upper part of a rice-paper tree (*Tetrapanax papyriferum*) showing the large leaves and the inflorescence. Rice paper is made by beating out the pith of the stem.

East Africa) and bagasse (the stalks of the sugarcane after the sugar has been extracted) are being developed.

A plant that has been of importance to man for a much longer period is the Giant Reed, *Arundo donax*. This giant perennial grass, which has a superficial resemblance to sugarcane, is a native of the countries around the Mediterranean Sea. For thousands of years, its stems provided hollow canes for the manufacture of musical instruments such as the panpipes of Greece. In addition, since at least 3000 B.C., it has provided the "reeds" for woodwind instruments. These "reeds" are small strips of the cane fixed so that, when blown air passes over them, they vibrate or beat against the mouthpiece of the instrument. Despite all of man's efforts through the ages, no better material has been found. *Arundo donax* is now cultivated around the world, for it also serves as an ornamental plant as well as a minor source of mat-making materials. At present, its potentiality as a prolific and easily grown source of industrial cellulose is being investigated, and in the future it may be used in paper-making (to the great relief of our forests). It may also help in controlling erosion by binding soil with its roots. Pressed board is also being made now from bagasse — the remains of sugarcane stems after the sugary juice has been expressed.

Paper-making today is highly scientific, and the process can be varied according to the product desired. However, although paper itself is produced in continuous sheets, the treatment of the pulp does not differ in principle from the process used in ancient times. As a preliminary, the wood chips are cooked with steam in chemical solutions called cooking liquors. Calcium bisulfite and sulfur dioxide are the commonest chemicals utilized for the manufacture of quality paper, but sodium hydroxide and mixtures of sodium hydroxide and sodium sulfide (for the manufacture of wrapping paper) have also been used. Unless the lignin is dissolved away by such means, only the crudest newsprint can be produced.

Rayon

A radical departure in the use of cellulose was made by nineteenth century chemists, who succeeded in dissolving cellulose by combining it with other chemicals (but without hydrolysis). Then they forced the solution through a spinneret (a group of fine nozzles) and hardened the filaments that resulted as the solvent evaporated. When twisted together, these filaments produced rayon thread, the first "artificial silk." Since the thread of all artificial silks is either cellulose itself or an ester of cellulose (usually the xanthate or acetate), they are not entirely "man-made" fibers.

Rayon production began in France in 1891, and grew so that it eventually rivalled the production of natural vegetable fibers such as cotton. More recently it has yielded in importance to purely synthetic polyester fibers such as nylon and Dacron, which have no connection with plant materials. However, with the increase in price of "petrochemical synthetics," the future looks brighter for more "natural" fibers.

If cellulose xanthate (viscose) is passed through a slit, rather than a spinneret, a thin sheet is produced. This can be hardened in an acid bath and later given a glycerin bath to make it flexible. The product is cellophane, a transparent wrapping material that revolutionized the marketing of food and other items where protection is needed but visibility of the goods is an important selling point. Now cellophane, in turn, has been largely replaced by synthetic transparent plastic sheets.

Plastics

The first plastic seems to have been Celluloid, made in 1869 by J. W. Hyatt, who treated cellulose with nitric acid (forming cellulose nitrate) and then combined the result with camphor. It remained virtually alone commercially until the end of the century. However, Celluloid is highly inflammable and has now been replaced by other plastic substances that do not derive from plants. Even in modern plastics, however, sawdust may retain a use as a "filler" in the plastic material.

Cellulose acetate is used in the manufacture of photographic film, since it is noninflammable, unlike the Celluloid formerly used for this purpose. The production of "artificial leather" by the combination of cellulose nitrate and castor oil was another development whose consequences have been far reaching, and it is very likely that both the cellulose and the lignin of wood will continue to play a part in the ever increasing range of plastics being evolved.

Cork

Cork, which makes up the outer part of the bark of all trees (see Fig. 12-2), has never played a major part in human history, but its supporting roles have been numerous and varied.

The first plant cells to be described were the cells of cork, which were observed under the microscope by Robert Hooke in 1665. They were the first because of the clarity of their appearance, which results from their regular arrangement (a product of their derivation from the cork cambium) and their lack of living contents when they are mature. It is to the air-filled state of cork cells and the impervious nature of their walls (which are impregnated with waterproof suberin) that cork owes its properties of flotability, insulation (against sound and heat), resilience, and impermeability to liquids and vapors. Because of these properties, cork has long been used by man in the manufacture of fishing floats (for lines and nets), insulating boards, shock absorbers, and, most familiarly, bungs and stoppers for casks and bottles. Adding to the value of cork in the last-mentioned use is its unreactive nature; the contents of a bottle are not deteriorated or altered in taste by contact with a cork stopper. And because cork is not damaged by contact with oil or grease, its use in the manufacture of gaskets is a relatively recent development of a comparable nature.

A cut cork surface exposes a multitude of tiny suction cups, for each cell that is cut across can act in this manner. Consequently, cork provides a nonslip surface that has been put to greatest use in the manufacture of linoleum. In this material, invented by the English manufacturer Frederick Walton in the

---

middle of the nineteenth century, ground cork is cooked with resins and linseed oil and spread on a burlap backing. Appropriate patterns can be printed on the surface before the final heat and pressure are applied.

Cork for all these purposes is produced by the cork oak, *Quercus suber*, a native of the countries around the western Mediterranean Sea. The bark is particularly thick on the trunk of this tree (a matter of some significance because it grows in hot, semi-arid conditions) and it may be peeled away in large sheets one to two inches thick. The peeling process, which is begun by making a longitudinal slit in the bark, may be repeated every ten years so long as care is taken not to damage the underlying cork cambium, from which regeneration must take place.

The cork bark of trees is penetrated at intervals by lenticels — areas in which the cork cells separate from each other and so permit the passage of gases. The presence of lenticels is vital to the tree if the underlying tissues are to continue to live. However, when cork is used for a bottle stopper, it is important that the cork sheet be cut in such a way that the lenticels run transversely rather than longitudinally through the stopper, so that the seal will be airtight.

It appears to have been the introduction of sparkling wines in the seventeenth century that led to the first use of cork stoppers for wine bottles at the Benedictine abbey of Hautvillers, in northern France. Previously, a wad of hemp dipped in oil had been used to stopper wine bottles. However, northern France is not a cork-producing area, and the industry developed in Spain. Today, Portugal produces the greatest amount of commercial cork, followed by the other Mediterranean countries. In California, some cork is produced from trees that were started from seed brought from the Old World.

13

The Utilization
of Drug Plants

From the very earliest times, plants have provided man with real or supposed means of healing. According to the anthropologist Carleton Coon, the religious practitioner, or shaman, was the first specialist—his is the oldest profession. He performed a medical and religious function, because disease among primitive peoples is usually equated with invasion of the body by evil spirits, and, consequently, religious incantations and rituals would be needed as an accompaniment to the administration of medicine. Without doubt, shamans existed in Late Paleolithic times. Although they accomplished many of their cures by "magical" means, they also had their stocks of herbs, which were used in the preparation of their potions. Medicine men and witch doctors play the same double role with unsophisticated peoples even today.

The medical botany of the Egyptians, Greeks, and Romans has already been referred to in Chapter 2, as well as the stagnation of this branch of science along with others during the Dark Ages. The production of "herbals" during the Middle Ages and their persistence in scarcely altered form into the nineteenth century has also been described.

Relatively few of the famous drug plants (the "botanicals") of earlier times continue to be employed as they were then. Even where their efficacy was real, it has been their fate to be replaced by other, more powerful drugs, which are often of synthetic origin. Nevertheless, plant parts are continuously coming to attention as the sources of new drugs, and serve in this manner until the chemical formulae of their active principles can be established and economical methods of synthesis found. Even this is not the final stage, which is the production by chemical substitution of synthetic drugs even more powerful than those that occur naturally.

One of the best-known drug plants is the opium poppy (*Papaver somniferum*), which was used as early as the second millennium B.C. More than 30 alkaloids are found in opium, the congealed latex derived from its fruit. Alkaloids are compounds of carbon, hydrogen, and oxygen with nitrogen (the latter in a "heterocyclic" ring with some of the carbon atoms) and a chemically basic reaction. Codeine and morphine are among the alkaloids in opium that have their place in medicine. Heroin is made by chemists from morphine. Cocaine, derived from the leaves of the coca tree (*Erythroxylon coca*) that grows in the Andes, has been replaced as a local anesthetic in dentistry by such related synthetics as procaine (Novacain). Even quinine, the alkaloid in the "wonder bark" from the jungles of Peru, is in the process of being replaced as an antimalarial agent by synthetic chemicals. And yet, all of these great natural drugs continue to be produced and used (and, in some cases, abused) on a worldwide scale.

Some of the other drugs derived from plants are glycosides (each a compound of a sugar with another, physiologically active, organic molecule).

Figure 13-1. Foxglove (*Digitalis purpurea*). From J. T. B. Syme, *Sowerby's English Botany*, 3rd ed. London: R. Hardwicke, 1863.

Digitalin, the heart stimulant from the leaves of the European foxglove (*Digitalis purpurea*) (Fig. 13-1) is of this kind.

Last, the euphoric active principles of marijuana, known in the Old World as hashish and derived from resinous hairs on the upper parts of pistillate plants of hemp (*Cannabis sativa*), are a series of complex alcohols, with tetrahydrocannabinols the most potent. They have now been synthesized.

In the sections that follow, a few of the most important drug plants have been chosen to illustrate a number of principles in the development of plants for civilized human beings.

Drug Plants of Temperate Origin

In addition to the mandrake (see Chapter 2), other members of the family Solanaceae have long been known to Europeans as producers of powerful drugs.

Belladonna (*Atropa belladonna*) is a perennial herb with ovate leaves, purplish flowers, and shiny black berries (Fig. 13-2). Its chief alkaloid, atropine, occurs in all parts of the plant and has many important medicinal uses as a stimulant to the sympathetic nervous system. Its action in dilating the pupil of the eye, which once made it popular with Spanish ladies as a means of giving sparkle to their eyes, has led to its employment as an adjunct to eye examination and surgery. It is also the basis of the plant name belladonna (meaning "beautiful woman").

Figure 13-2.   Belladonna (*Atropa belladonna*), the source of atropine. From J. T. B. Syme, *Sowerby's English Botany*, 3rd ed. London: R. Hardwicke, 1863.

Ginseng, now derived from the fleshy roots of *Panax quinquefolium*, a herb of the Araliaceae, is a product of the forests of eastern North America. It has limited use in this continent, but is greatly valued as a cure for almost every illness in China, to which country its export has been a significant item of trade in past years. There it replaces diminished supplies of the local drug plant *Panax ginseng*. The real utility of ginseng as a drug is subject to some doubt, based as it is to some extent on the supposed resemblance of the ginseng root to the human figure (the age-old "doctrine of signs"). It contains at least one glycoside (panaquilon).

The alkaloid ephedrine comes from the leafless bushes of the genus *Ephedra*, which occur in arid regions of the world. The Chinese species, *E. sinica*, has been particularly utilized. Ephedrine causes the contraction of mucous membranes, which is the basis of its use in nose drops and inhalants. It also acts as a stimulant. It has been synthesized and also, to some extent, replaced by other synthetic alkaloids with closely related structures. A related alkaloid, pseudo-ephedrine, is obtained by making an infusion of the dried stems and flowers of western North American species of *Ephedra*; this stimulant was a constituent of the so-called "Mormon" or "Mexican" tea, drunk by pioneers in the American West.

Drug Plants of Tropical Origin

Cinchona

The story of cinchona bark and its alkaloids such as quinine, is in many ways similar to the story of rubber. Although now mostly grown in Indonesia, the genus *Cinchona* (Rubiaceae) is native to tropical America, particularly at elevations above 1,000 feet in Peru and Bolivia. More than one species is involved, but all are evergreen trees that are usually cross-pollinated, and natural hybridization has contributed to the mixing of their characters (Fig. 13-3).

The antimalarial properties of the bark were discovered about 1638, when it supposedly cured a fever of the Countess of Chinchon, wife of the Viceroy of Peru. It was carried to Spain where its reputation grew. Outside of Spain, its reputation as a cure for malaria took longer to become established, but when it was successfully used to cure King Charles II of England and then members of the French and Spanish royal families later in the seventeenth century, the efficacy of the "fever bark" was appreciated. In the eighteenth century, Linnaeus named the genus after the Countess (without spelling her name quite correctly).

The bark was obtained from the felling of wild trees until the mid-nineteenth century. Then the Dutch and British governments sent expeditions to collect seeds in the South American jungles in order to establish plantations in southeast Asia. The seed which the British expedition collected was from *Cinchona succirubra* (so-called "red bark"), and was taken to India, where plants of this species are now used as a rootstock upon which other species may be grafted.

Charles Ledger, an English resident in Bolivia, also sent seeds of *Cinchona* to Europe, and half of these were bought by a planter in Sri Lanka, the other half going to the Dutch government for a total payment equivalent to slightly more than $500. From Ledger's seed, the *Cinchona* plantations in Java were started, and they now produce 90 per cent of the world export trade in quinine. *C. ledgeriana*, the species involved, gives the highest yields of quinine, some selected strains producing up to 16 per cent in the bark. Other species that have been used are *C. officinalis* and *C. calisaya*.

Figure 13-3. Inflorescence of Cinchona (*Cinchona sp.*), the fever ("wonder") bark tree. Drawing by Charles Marie de la Condamine, *Memoires de l'Académie Royale des Sciences*, 1738.

During World War II, when East Indian supplies of quinine were cut off, the procurement of native *Cinchona* bark in South America again became a matter of great importance, and a number of famous botanists led expeditions to locate sources of the drug. The war also stimulated research on the production of synthetic substitutes for quinine, and progress in this field has continued even though plantation-grown supplies of quinine have returned to the world market. It may be expected that malaria ultimately will be treated exclusively with synthetic drugs.

Curare

Curare is another product of the tropical American jungle. Indians in its native area have long prepared it from mysterious brews of barks, seeds, and herbs, the purpose of which was to make poisons for the tips of arrows and blowpipe darts. For a long time, the major constituent of these brews was believed to be strychnine, from the seeds and bark of *Strychnos* spp. (Logania-ceae). However, in 1938, Richard Gill, who lived with and won the confidence of the Indians, showed that the active principle came from the leaves of *Chon-dodendron tomentosum* (Menispermaceae). The alkaloid was isolated in 1939 and named d-tubocurarine. Tubocurarine interferes with the transmission of nerve impulses to the skeletal muscles, but can do this only if it is injected into the bloodstream (as in an arrow wound!). This alkaloid is now used to treat rabies and lockjaw and for the relaxation of muscles in surgery and in spastic conditions.

Steroid Sources

One biochemical group of substances that has been recognized in recent years to be of great importance to man is the steroids. These substances, all of which contain the basic 17-carbon ring structure shown in Figure 13-4,

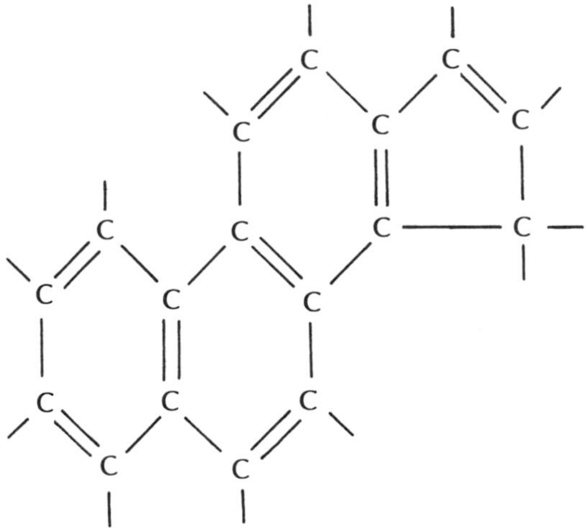

Figure 13-4. The 17-carbon, 4-ring center of all steroid molecules.

occur naturally in plant and animal tissues; many animal hormones (including some human ones) belong to this group. Thus, cortisone (which raises the blood-sugar level by stimulating the conversion of amino acids to carbohydrates and, as a consequence, has many medical uses) is a member of the group, as are several sex hormones.

Cortisone is a secretion from the cortex of the adrenal glands. It was isolated in 1935 and synthesized from the bile acids of cattle in 1944. But 40 animals were needed to produce a day's supply for one person. Consequently, richer and cheaper sources of substances capable of conversion into cortisone were sought. After an investigation of the African arrow poison sarmentogenin, derived from the seeds of shrubs of the genus *Strophanthus* (Apocynaceae), attention was directed towards the monocotyledonous families, Dioscoreaceae and Agavaceae.

Plants of these families contain saponins which consist of a sugar in combination with a sapogenin. Sapogenins are chemically quite closely related to steroids.

An American chemist, R. E. Marker, led the way in the utilization of the underground rhizomes produced by the Mexican species of the yam genus *Dioscorea* to produce steroids in commercial quantities (see Fig. 13-5). Diosgenin, a saponin in the cytoplasm of cells in these rhizomes, can be converted into cortisone, into the male hormone testosterone, and into female hormones (estrogens as well as progesterone). Cortisone's many potential uses include allaying the symptoms of numerous serious ailments (especially rheumatoid arthritis), and the female hormones are used in contraceptive pills. As a result, the demand for these derivatives of plant products has skyrocketed; the supply of naturally collected yam rhizomes from Mexico is inadequate to provide the quantities of sapogenins that are required. Other plant sources of steroid precursors will probably be found. Agaves and yuccas may be collected but, in the future, the soybean will probably figure prominently because it contains appropriate chemicals and can be cultivated easily on a large scale. In addition, synthetic steroids are now utilized, particularly in the manufacture of contraceptive pills.

Drug Plants of Importance to Mental Health

Rauvolfia

In India, shrubs of the genus *Rauvolfia* (Apocynaceae) have been known since antiquity as medical agents, and were used in the treatment of a great variety of afflictions (Fig. 13-6). The name of this genus is often misspelled

---

Figure 13-5. A young *Dioscorea* vine. Grown at University of California Botanical Garden.

Rauwolfia. In 1931, Indian research workers reported that alkaloids from this genus had real promise for the alleviation of the more violent kinds of insanity and, two years later, their value in reducing blood pressure was demonstrated. However, it was another 21 years before reserpine, the active principle from the roots of *Rauvolfia,* was isolated and the drug could be used systematically as a tranquilizer and for relief of hypertension (high blood pressure). Now *Rauvolfia serpentina,* the source plant, is cultivated in plantations, and other species of the genus are also being grown and used. Although reserpine has been synthesized, it is still manufactured from these natural sources.

Figure 13-6. A young shrub of *Rauvolfia*, the genus that contains snake root (*R. serpentina*), the source of the drug reserpine. Grown at University of California Botanical Garden.

Psychoactive Drugs

The Spanish explorers of northern Mexico and southwestern Texas found the Indians eating, in ritual fashion, slices from "buttons" of what was called *peyotl*. These buttons of peyotl (or peyote) are actually derived from the small, cylindrical, spineless cactus *Lophophora williamsii*, which grows with only its button-like top exposed above ground (Fig. 13-7). The buttons have a most unpleasant taste, but produce hallucinations in which lavish kaleidoscopic displays of color are often seen.

Although banned by the Spaniards, the use of peyote has persisted to the present time as part of the religious rituals of some American Indians. In certain states its consumption is permitted in restricted circumstances; in others it has been prohibited altogether. Since 1918 it has been used in the ceremonial rites of the Native American Church. Chemical analysis of peyote has revealed the presence of at least nine alkaloids, and the most important of these, mescaline, has been synthesized. Under strict medical control it can be used in the treatment of schizophrenia.

The medical qualities of a number of other hallucinogens of plant origin are being investigated for their potential value in the study and treatment of mental diseases. One of these is lysergic acid, derived from "ergot," the spore-pro-

Figure 13-7. Whole plant of peyote (*Lophophora williamsii*) dug from the soil. When growing, only the "button" shows above the soil level.

ducing reproductive body (the sclerotium) of the fungus *Claviceps purpurea* (Fig. 13-8), which infects many grasses and cereals (particularly rye) and has been the cause of many past disasters when accidentally incorporated in food. Crude ergot causes severe muscle spasms and gangrene, as well as mental reactions, but in modern medicine its properties are put to good use in controlled fashion. Even in earlier times it was used in dilute form by midwives to accelerate labor in childbirth. Since 1943, related drugs have been synthesized, including d-lysergic acid diethylamide (LSD).

The history of certain toadstool fungi is much like that of peyote. The fly-agaric (*Amanita muscaria*) was used by Siberian tribes that inhabited the Kamchatka Peninsula. After the ritual consumption of small quantities of this narcotic fungus, first seen by an explorer in 1730, the tribesmen were supposedly capable of extraordinary feats of strength. In Mexico, another kind of toadstool, *Psilocybe mexicana*, has been used as a hallucinogen by Indians for thousands of years. The active principle, psilocybin, has now been isolated and may have real medical value. It was successfully produced synthetically in 1958.

Other hallucinogens are derived from flowering plants in the Solanaceae (particularly alkaloids from the genera *Datura* and *Methysticodendron*), the Convolvulaceae (where amides of lysergic acid occur in the Morning Glory genus *Ipomoea* and in the related genus *Rivea*), and a number of other families.

Figure 13-8. Inflorescence of rye (*Secale cereale*) bearing several ripe fruiting bodies (sclerotia) of ergot (*Claviceps purpurea*).

Lower Plants as Drug Sources

Quite the most dramatic utilization of plants as drug sources in the twentieth century has been the development of antibiotics, substances that are produced and excreted by living organisms in the course of their metabolism and that are capable of killing other organisms. Most of the producers of antibiotics that have been utilized by man are fungi, actinomycetes, and bacteria (particularly soil bacteria), and they have been put to use in the fight against disease-producing bacteria (very few of them having any effect on viruses).

The story of Sir Alexander Fleming's observation in 1928 of the antibiotic action of a fungal contaminant — actually *Penicillium notatum* — on a culture of the bacterium *Staphylococcus* is well known (Fig. 13-9). He discovered that the action was due to a chemical excreted by the fungus during its growth, and demonstrated that the antibiotic, which he called penicillin, was not toxic to animals.

Nevertheless, the extraction and concentration of penicillin had to wait a number of years, until the emergency of war accelerated the effort to understand its chemistry and produce it on a large scale. To begin with, penicillin was used as a filtrate of the liquid medium on which the fungus had grown, but, during World War II, processes of extraction and purification were perfected and a stable crystalline product was obtained. Penicillin has now been synthesized.

Historically, it is worthy of note that as long ago as 1877 Pasteur and Joubert observed that the growth of anthrax bacteria was slowed down by the presence of other organisms; and in 1889 Emmerich and Löw isolated from the bacterium *Pseudomonas aeruginosa* a substance that served this function. They called their antibiotic substance pyocyanase.

Figure 13-9. Cultures of *Penicillium chrysogenum* growing on an agar plate. This fungus is now the source of almost all of the world's supply of penicillin. Reproduced by courtesy of Chas. Pfizer & Co., Inc.

An increasing range of antibiotics is now being prepared from various micro-organisms. They are effective because they interfere with the metabolic processes of the pathogenic bacteria against which they are used. However, these must be metabolic processes peculiar to bacteria; if the same processes occur in human beings, the antibiotics will be toxic to man as well as bacteria and will be useless in medicine.

It is impossible to estimate the magnitude of the effect of penicillin and other antibiotics on the life and health of man in the second half of the twentieth century. Relief from many diseases (although not all) is a great blessing, yet the situation is complicated by problems such as the spread, through selection, of virulent strains of the disease-causing bacteria that are resistant to the antibiotic. These new factors in man's fight against disease would provide subject matter sufficient for a whole book.

Tobacco

When Columbus's sailors landed in the West Indies in 1492, they saw Carib Indians smoking tobacco. The Indians used tobacco in two ways: first by rolling it and smoking it as cigars, and second by burning the dried leaves on a fire and inhaling the smoke through hollow reeds stuck into their nostrils. It is said that these reeds, or the cigars, were called *tobacos*, and the name has been transferred to the substance that is smoked.

The Spaniards introduced cigars to Spain in 1519, and the use of tobacco for smoking, chewing, and as snuff spread rapidly through southern Europe and the Middle East. Tobacco first reached England in 1573 when Sir John Hawkins (seadog and sometime pirate) carried it there from Florida. Sir Walter Raleigh, by his example of pipe smoking, did much to popularize the habit in England. However, in 1603, King James I issued a pamphlet entitled "A Counterblaste to Tobacco," in which he attributed many harmful consequences to the habit of smoking. In an attempt to stamp out tobacco, he placed a heavy duty on its importation.

This pioneering taxation of tobacco and tobacco products set a fashion that has been followed all over the world, and although it has conspicuously failed to halt the spread of smoking, it has provided tremendous revenues. The Colony of Virginia, which had been founded in 1607, pinned its faith to the growing of the tobacco plant on a plantation scale, and, in the early years of the colony, tobacco was even used for money (as it later was in Maryland).

Cultivated tobacco plants belong to two species, *Nicotiana tabacum* and *N. rustica*, the former being of overwhelmingly greater importance (Fig. 13-10). Neither species is known wild.

Nicotiana tabacum appears to have arisen from the hybridization of two wild South American species (*N. sylvestris* and, in all probability, *N. tomentosiformis*), followed by the doubling of the chromosome number in the sterile hybrid. *N. rustica* is also polyploid and of South American origin, spreading in pre-Columbian times throughout Central America to eastern North America. Although grown for smoking tobacco in some areas (particularly during colonial times), the greatest use of *N. rustica* has been as a source of nicotine for insecticides. For the best yields of nicotine (up to nine per cent), it must be grown in a rather temperate environment. By contrast, the best smoking varieties of *N. tabacum* contain only a little more than one per cent nicotine.

Interestingly enough, none of the wild species that are possible parents of *Nicotiana tabacum* contains any appreciable quantity of nicotine in the mature leaves. In fact, these species possess genes that cause the destruction of the small quantities present in immature leaves. D. U. Gerstel has pointed out that if the first cultivated tobacco received these genes (in double dose) from its parental wild species and yet was liked by man for its nicotine content, this must mean that immature leaves were used. Later, when strains were developed in which the inactivation of nicotine does not occur, maturing of the leaves as currently practiced became possible.

Nicotiana tabacum is a stout annual or short-lived perennial plant that

Figure 13-10. Plants of (left) *Nicotiana tabacum* and (right) *N. rustica.* Grown in University of California Botanical Garden.

grows up to seven feet in height. It is propagated from an extremely tiny seed, which may retain its viability for as long as 20 years. On tobacco plantations, the seed beds are usually protected by artificial shading, and the seedlings are not planted out in the fields until they are several inches high. When the required number of leaves (less than 20) has been produced on the plants in the field, these are "topped." This stops further growth in height, prevents flowering, and causes an enlargement of the existing leaves, with an accumulation in them of chemicals (including nicotine).

Individual leaves or whole stems are then harvested and dried. Curing follows, and may be performed in one of three ways: (1) air curing (in well-ventilated barns), (2) flue curing (with artificial heat), or (3) fire curing (in the smoke of slow fires). Some fermentation as well as drying occurs at this stage. Cured leaves are sorted and usually sold in this condition. Later they are "aged," a longer fermentation process carried out in boxes or casks and lasting for months or years. During this second fermentation, the aroma develops to a maximum and other chemical changes, including a decrease in nicotine content, take place.

In the United States—the largest producer of tobacco—different geographic regions are concerned with the growing of tobacco varieties for special purposes. The Connecticut Valley growers, for example, grow plants under cheesecloth tents to produce large, thin leaves to be used as cigar wrappers and binders. Flue-cured leaves suitable for cigarette tobacco are produced in enormous quantities in North and South Carolina, Georgia, Virginia, Florida, and Alabama, as well as some other states. Dark, fire-cured tobaccos for pipe mixtures and snuff are especially associated with Virginia, Kentucky, and Tennessee.

There is evidence that heavy tobacco smoking may promote respiratory diseases, heart troubles, and the incidence of lung cancer, but whatever may be the future of tobacco for smoking, there is little doubt that it will not disappear overnight. Tobacco is a habit-forming drug, and a sufficiently high proportion of the world's population is addicted to ensure that government revenues will not suffer significant depreciation from loss of the many taxes on the "weed" for some time to come.

14

Tanning and Decoration with Dyes

In this chapter we shall be concerned with a variety of substances that can be extracted from plant parts and used by man for the treatment and decoration of his clothing. These substances include tannins, which man has used from a very early date to prepare leather from the animal skins that formed his first covering, as well as plant dyestuffs, which he used for coloring skins (his own and those of the animals that he captured) and the textiles that he was able to manufacture later.

Tannins

The group of chemical substances known as tannins includes a variety of materials formed by the metabolic breakdown of sugars; their common features include their great astringency, their chemical reducing nature, and their solubility in water. In the plants that produce them, they tend to accumulate in places where they do not interfere with further metabolism, such as the heartwood of a tree trunk or the cork bark that surrounds the trunk. Here, not only are they out of the way of living tissues but also they can perform a valuable protective function, that of resisting decay.

The reducing nature of tannins is put to use in civilized life in two ways.

They are used to combine with the proteins in skins to produce leather (thereby increasing the resistance of these skins to decay and to wear), and they are also used in the manufacture of inks. The second use, of course, is a much more recent one.

Tannins are produced from a number of tree sources, usually from the bark. In temperate regions, oaks, chestnuts and other large trees have been much used. Unfortunately, the North American chestnut (*Castanea dentata*), which was once extremely valuable as a source of tannin, has now been almost completely eliminated by the chestnut blight disease (caused by a fungus, *Endothia parasitica*, introduced from eastern Asia at the beginning of the twentieth century). Tannin is extracted from the wood of dead trees, but obviously this supply cannot last. Consequently, at the present time in North America, species of hemlock spruce (*Tsuga canadensis* and *T. heterophylla*) are the most important indigenous sources of tannin-producing bark, with tan-bark oak (*Lithocarpus densiflora*) being of some local significance in California.

In South America, the wood of quebracho (*Schinopsis lorentzii*, of the Anacardiaceae) provides the greatest supply of tannins from tree wood. In South Africa and Australia, many species of *Acacia* are deliberately grown in plantations (as "Wattles") to provide tannin materials from their bark. Around the world, in tropical regions, mangrove trees (*Rhizophora* spp.), which often form almost impenetrable forests standing in brackish water at the mouths of the larger rivers, are useful sources. Their resistance to animal attack (due to the tannins that copiously impregnate them) has also led to the utilization of their trunks as piles in the making of jetties and other marine constructions.

In the present century, other reducing substances have been produced which can fulfill many of the uses previously performed by tannins, but they still have great importance in leather manufacture.

Dyestuffs

Some trees and many herbs produce dyestuffs, and until relatively recently the bulk of the world's dyes were produced from plant sources. Unquestionably the use of dyes to modify man's appearance began very early in his history; one can very easily imagine its origin in accidental staining from berries or other plant parts. The deliberate use of these plant extracts to produce a color probably followed soon after. We know that primitive man used plant dyes (along with mineral pigments) to color various parts of his body during religious and warlike occasions, and, as soon as he came to use clothes, it was inevitable that he should endeavor to relieve the drabness of their appearance by decorating them with color.

One of the most ancient plant dyes is woad, which is obtained from an herbaceous member of the family Cruciferae (*Isatis tinctoria*), originally native in extreme eastern Europe. Woad spread through Europe in prehistoric times.

Although the Greeks and Romans knew of this plant as a medicinal herb, it was when the latter invaded Britain, just before the beginning of the Christian era, that they found the warriors who resisted them had covered themselves with the dye derived from it, in the hope that by painting their bodies blue they would scare their opponents. From the direct use of woad on the human body, its use spread to that of a textile dye. From Roman times onward, the woad plant was extensively cultivated, first in England and France and, later, in what is now called Germany. By the mid-thirteenth century, the manufacture of woad had acquired such importance that it was internationally controlled.

In the fresh condition, a bath of woad gives a deep blue, even black coloration to cloth, but this becomes weakened by use, and older baths produce a very clear blue color. This dye, which was the standard source of blue coloring for many years, could be used alone or in combination with other dyes. Thus, the famous Saxon green (especially remembered in connection with the exploits of Robin Hood in Sherwood Forest) was obtained by staining cloth blue with woad and then yellow with a dye obtained from the Wild Mignonette, *Reseda luteola* (of the family Resedaceae).

The woad plant is a biennial herb producing, in its first year of growth, simply a rosette of more or less ovate leaves. In its second year, a flowering stem is produced from the rosette and may grow as high as four or five feet from the ground, bearing large panicles of small, yellow, mustard-like flowers (Fig. 14-1).

The dyestuff itself is provided by the leaves of the woad plant. These were picked by hand and piles of leaves were then crushed under heavy wooden rollers drawn by horses. After crushing, the material was hand-kneaded into balls. This process stained the hands of the operatives black, and it was completely impossible to remove the coloration by washing; it was necessary to wait for the formation of new skin for recovery. In the Middle Ages, every trade had its hazard and left its indelible mark on its followers, and it is one symptom of the progress of our civilization that these hazards have been reduced so that discrimination of this sort has been almost eliminated.

The balls of crushed leaves were dried on trays and could then be stored. Later, when it was desired to make dye, the balls had to be fermented or couched in "couching houses." Here the balls were ground to powder by rollers and then piled into layers up to three feet thick. These were wetted and allowed to ferment for several weeks, the pile being turned with spades at

---

Figure 14-1. Drawing of parts of a shoot and an inflorescence of woad (*Isatis tinctoria*), together with isolated fruits. From J. T. B. Syme, *Sowerby's English Botany*, 3rd ed. London: R. Hardwicke, 1863.

intervals. The fermentation produced heat causing the piles to steam and develop a foul odor. So noxious was the smell that Queen Elizabeth of England, in the sixteenth century, gave an order that no woad growing or processing should take place within five miles of any one of her residences. After couching, the woad material could again be dried, and this represents another stage at which the material could be stored. In this state the material contained insoluble indigotine, the dyestuff itself.

When it was finally needed, the dyer wetted the woad material and allowed further fermentation to occur. This process reduced the insoluble indigotine into soluble indigo white, and it was in a solution of this that the fabric was steeped. Even so, there was no blue color; it was only when the fabric was taken out of the dye bath and allowed to dry that the indigo white oxidized to indigotine and the full blue color was obtained. It is surprising that such a complicated process of dye production and use should have been discovered and worked out between prehistoric times and medieval times by men whose cultural development we have not otherwise thought of as being very great. Nevertheless, the process as conceived by them became standard for many centuries.

Indigo

The blue pigment from woad is indigotine. The same pigment can be produced by other plants that are taxonomically unrelated to woad. These plants belong to the genus *Indigofera* (of the family Leguminosae), and the species frequently involved in dye production are *I. arrecta* from Africa and *I. sumatrana* and *I. tinctoria* from tropical Asia (Fig. 14-2). It will be noticed that one of these species has the same specific name as the woad plant, signifying its use in dyeing. In *Indigofera,* as in *Isatis,* the precursor of indigotine actually present in the plants is the glycoside indican.

Indigo plants have been known in Asia for more than 4,000 years, and their generic name is derived from the Latin word *indicum,* indicating that the plants came from India itself. They are herbs or small shrubs, with pinnate leaves and dull reddish-purple flowers, each having the characteristic butterfly shape of flowers in the Leguminosae. When these plants are used as a source of indigotine, the dyestuff is again obtained from the leaves.

Indigo plants were known to Europeans from an early date, but their importation into woad-producing countries was successfully blocked until the

Figure 14-2.   A shoot of Indigofera, the genus that produces the dyestuff indigotine.

seventeenth century by the "woadites," an international group of woad producers who wielded a powerful political influence. Eventually, indigo supplanted woad, but not until after the opening of a sea route from India to Europe around the Cape of Good Hope and after a bitter fight had been waged. However, indigo could not be grown in England, France, or Germany, and therefore in the early years of British occupation of India the importation of indigo was one of the activities of the East India Company. Subsequently, the Indian trade declined because of competition from indigo production on plantations that had been set up in the Carolinas and Georgia. Later still, however, when large-scale cotton and tobacco growing became the principal agricultural activities of the Southern states, the emphasis on indigo growing shifted back to India.

In dyeing with indigo, the stems and leaves are crushed and then steeped in water for 12 hours. Fermentations occur (and these may be aided by the addition of woad leaves, which provide the right enzyme for the conversion of insoluble indigotine to indigo white). After this, the solution (containing indigo white) is aerated by beaters until a blue color develops. The process is then stopped and indigotine is precipitated; this may be later used in a separate bath for dyeing cloth.

Indigotine was the standard blue dye until 1856, when an English chemist, W. H. Perkin, in trying to make a synthetic quinine from coal tar, produced a synthetic dye. This dye he called mauve; it was the first of the aniline dyes that have now virtually completely supplanted natural dyes. Indigotine itself was synthesized in 1880 from coal-tar products by Adolf von Bayer, in Germany. However, it was not until the end of the nineteenth century that the synthetic indigotine was produced more cheaply than the natural dyestuff.

Annatto (*Achiote*)

Just as woad was used by the ancient Britons to stain their bodies blue, anhatto, a red dye, reputedly was used by the Caribbean Indians for the same warlike purpose.

Annatto is derived from a small tree or shrub, *Bixa orellana*, a member of the Bixaceae. Originally native in northern South America, in Central America, and in the Caribbean region, this shrub is now spread all around the tropics. It bears pinkish flowers (Fig. 14-3), and these in turn produce spiny fruits that contain red seeds surrounded by a red pulp (Fig. 14-4). The seeds and pulp, when extracted with an organic solvent, produce the dye. It is obtained in pure form by evaporating the solvent to a paste. The dyestuff is not soluble in water, but can be dissolved in fat solvents as well as in fats and oils themselves, and the Caribbean Indians used a solution in animal fat in smearing annatto on the body. It is interesting that this kind of use persists, for annatto is one of the red

Figure 14-3. Young bush of annatto (*Bixa orellana*) in flower. Grown at University of California Botanical Garden.

Figure 14-4. Spiny fruits of annatto (*Bixa orellana*), one of which has opened to disclose the red seeds, set in a red (arillate) pulp from which the dyestuff is obtained. Photograph by W. H. Hodge from Ward's Natural Science Establishment, Inc. Reproduced by permission.

coloring matters in lipstick, as well as being much used for coloring cheese, butter, and margarine.

Henna

Another coloring material important in cosmetics is henna, an orange dye obtained from the leaves of *Lawsonia inermis* (Lythraceae), a shrub long culti- vated in India, Arabia, and Egypt. Henna was used by women in ancient Egypt for tinting their hands reddish-brown; at present its major use is in coloring rinses for the hair and for dyeing leather.

Cochineal

There are many other stories associated with dyes that could be quoted, for, by reason of human vanity and color consciousness, they have played an important role in history. However, one of the most fascinating of these con- cerns cochineal, a dyestuff that is obtained not from a plant but from an insect that feeds on plants. The cochineal insect (of the genus *Dactylopius*) is a para- site of prickly pear cacti, *Opuntia* and related genera, in Mexico (Fig. 14-5). The brilliant red cochineal dye was extracted from the bodies of these insects by the Aztecs, and the Spanish conquerors, observing this and approving of it, established the industry in the Canary Islands by introducing there both the cacti and the insects.

Figure 14-5. A large prickly pear (*Opuntia robusta*) from Mexico, bearing fruits on the flattened succulent stems. The spines are modified leaves. University of California Botani- cal Garden.

It is reported that a Governor of New South Wales, Captain Arthur Phillip, while on his way with the first colonists to take up his duties in 1787, saw the cochineal industry in the Canary Islands and decided that it would be suitable for the Australian economy. Therefore, he picked up cacti and insects and carried them to Australia.

Unfortunately, whereas the cactus flourished in Australia, the cochineal insect did not, and the industry was a failure. Prickly pear cacti, however, which were also introduced as ornamentals and hedge plants, became one of the worst pests of the country, dominating large areas of grazing land in Queensland, New South Wales, and Victoria. Being so heavily armoured with spines (modified leaves) on their flattened succulent stems, the cacti were not eaten by cattle, and, additionally, they prevented the cattle from eating such grass as survived between the cactus plants. In 1925, 60,000,000 acres were affected, half of them so badly that the land was rendered useless. This pest was ultimately controlled in Australia by the introduction from Mexico of other cactus parasites, which help to keep the prickly pear cacti from being a nuisance there. In particular, a moth (*Cactoblastis cactorum*), whose larvae feed on the prickly pear, was introduced, and it cleared off huge areas of prickly pear with amazing speed. The defeat of the prickly pear in Australia is one of the best examples of "biological control" of an introduced pest, and, as such, gives us real hope for the future extension of this kind of applied biology.

Even though vegetable dyes are no longer important in human economy, they still have a "folk art" interest and it is fitting that we should remember their prominent role in human history. Next time we are upset by the accidental staining of our clothes with fruit juices, it might be well to remember that during the greater part of human history this was an event that was deliberately contrived.

15

The Future of Plants
in Relation to Humanity

In this final chapter it will be our purpose to attempt some forecast of the relation of plants to humanity in the future. Although we do hear that we live in the "Atomic Era" or the "Space Age," and even though our children tend to grow up in cities where they may see none of the usual and obvious aspects of the dependence of human beings upon plants, still there is practically no weakening of the bond that unites us to the plants. Even if we buy our food wrapped and processed from a supermarket, the energy stored up in it is still acquired by the old-fashioned process of photosynthesis, in which the sun's radiated energy is captured by plants through the intervention of their chlorophyll. Great may be the uses of atomic energy, but so far they show no signs of including the provision of energy for living processes, and it seems that people will be dependent on plants directly and indirectly for as far into the future as human imagination can be projected. Even if artificial — "in vitro" — photosynthesis is developed, it will be a very long time before this process could provide for the ever expanding population of humanity on the earth's surface.

Food Production

Although all of the other relations of plants to man will continue in the future, those which bear some relation to the provision of food must have the greatest attention because the "population explosion" is probably the biggest challenge facing human beings now and in the foreseeable future. It is estimated that, unless checks are imposed on a scale far beyond anything now operative, the four billion population of the world today will have become six or seven billion by the year 2000.

Even without this enormously increased demand on food supplies, it must be remembered that famine is no stranger in the world today (where over three and a half million people are likely to die of starvation every year). Undisputed estimates indicate that over half of the world's population is undernourished or improperly nourished. Is there any hope that food production can be increased sufficiently to feed the increased population that is inevitable even if the birth rate is slowed down? Is it possible that this food can be produced without devoting the whole of the earth's surface to its production? After all, there are esthetics to be considered even apart from the potential dangers inherent in devoting all our resources to a single end. Can such a rate of food production be maintained without complete exhaustion of soil, water, atmospheric and energy-supplying resources? And how can this be achieved with no more social upheaval in the world than is desirable on grounds of human dignity and well-being?

Even though satisfactory answers to these questions are not yet available, and pessimism may be more justifiable than optimism, it behooves us to try to achieve the international cooperation and scientific planning necessary to, at least, reduce the impact of overpopulation and environmental deterioration.

Two lines of attack may be followed: first, we may attempt to increase significantly the yields from conventional agriculture; second, we may adopt unconventional means of producing food materials. A start has been made on each line.

Improvement of Conventional Crops

In 1962 the International Rice Research Institute was opened at Los Baños, in the Philippines. A joint effort of U.S. philanthropic foundations and the Philippine government, the Institute has shown the way to a dramatic improvement in the yields of paddy rice in southeast Asia. By making the difficult cross between selected "japonica" and "indica" races, scientists at the IRRI have been able to raise the potential productivity of a form of dwarf rice with acceptable grain characteristics by more than 700 per cent. This rice does not "lodge" even when heavily fertilized. Breeding of varieties appropriate to tropical America is now being carried out at the International Center of Tropical Agriculture (CIAT) in Colombia. With the inclusion in these breeding programs of an emphasis on resistance to diseases and pests and of tolerance to a wider range of environmental conditions, as well as some mechanization of the agricultural operations, the yield of rice in tropical paddies may now approach

8,000 pounds per acre under optimal conditions. However, conditions are not always optimal, and in some climatic circumstances, when abundant fertilizer and machines are not available and technical information is not passed on to the farmer, yields may not be much better than with the traditional varieties of rice.

A similar story could be told from Mexico where, in addition to the revolution in wheat production (Chapter 5), an enormous increase in maize yields was made possible by the breeding and husbandry research program at the International Maize and Wheat Improvement Center (CIMMYT) in Chapingo, near Mexico City. Maize production in Mexico (its home), increased threefold between 1943 and 1965. The protein quality of maize the world over may be expected to improve with the incorporation of genes for increased lysine content (Chapter 6).

Further spectacular increases in wheat and maize yields in countries like Mexico may not be possible, however, because the limit in easily cultivated (or irrigable) land may have been reached. In the future, emphasis may have to be placed on farming drier, more marginal lands, and, as a consequence, cereal crops such as sorghum may increase in importance. Improved varieties of sorghum, which include a higher lysine content, are already being produced, but an interesting complication has arisen. Improved grain quality in sorghum includes a reduction in the bitter tannins of the seed coat, but these tannins are deterrents to birds. With a reduction, the birds can take a heavy toll of the grain before it is harvested. An appropriate compromise must be reached.

This is one small illustration of the kind of problem that has to be faced in bringing what has been called the "Green Revolution" to fruition. A prime requirement for the present and the future is research to find means of adapting the new varieties and the techniques for handling them so they benefit the way of life of the small farmers who form the majority of rural inhabitants in the tropics.

The Need for More Protein

The situation in regard to starchy foods in most of the world is not in itself disastrous, and increased cereal production by means such as those described above may be able to take care of the carbohydrate needs of the increased population in the next decade or two. The desperate shortage, which cannot fail to become even worse, is that of protein. Cattle diseases such as trypanosomiasis may be responsible for the nonutilization of many grassland areas in the tropics of the Old World, but even if these diseases were eliminated, the ever-expanding need for protein by human beings would still not be met. Unconventional approaches to the production of protein for human consumption are called for.

Drastic reevaluation of the ways in which we use growing space is necessary. After all, it is not a very efficient means of agriculture to raise plants to feed animals and then eat only some portions of the animals to gain the protein so vital to our existence. The pig is generally considered one of the most efficient converters of plant protein into meat among domesticated animals, but less than 20 per cent of the plant material which the pig consumes is converted into meat. And even if we were to eat the whole animal, we should still not utilize all of the energy stored in it. The Second Law of Thermodynamics implies that every time energy is transferred from one chemical to another, some of it is irretrievably lost. There is no way of avoiding this loss except by cutting out the steps.

If we should switch our attention from the raising of protein in animal form to the direct utilization of plant proteins, what plants and plant parts should we use? The two richest sources are seeds, where protein reserves are laid down, and the parts of the plant where protein (or at least amino acid) manufacture is going on. The latter are especially rich if they are also centers of growth, which means that leaves are often rich in protein. Both seeds and leaves are worthy of closer examination as sources of protein-rich food.

Oil Seed Cake

The cake left behind when the oil is squeezed out of the seeds of such plants as soybean, peanut, and cotton has long been used as fertilizer or animal feed because of its high protein content. Now this cake is being pressed into service as a human foodstuff. The amino acids present often include good proportions of those needed to complement the amino acids in cereal grains. There have been reasons why these cakes have not previously been used to the fullest extent—soybean cake contains an anti-trypsin principle; cotton seed cake contains toxic gossypol; and stored peanuts can be attacked by a very toxic fungus, *Aspergillus flavus*. Now that methods of removing these substances are available, there need be no impediment to the use of the cake. Also, plant breeders have produced cotton plants that lack the gossypol-producing glands and a patent has been taken out for the production of protein-rich bread containing this cotton oil seed cake. Generally, for human nutrition, oil seed cake is used in combination with other foodstuffs such as maize flour, sorghum flour, yeast, etc. Several preparations of this sort are being used experimentally in tropical countries.

Oil seed cake often has a rather strong flavor that can prejudice its acceptance as food, and increasing attention is being given to extracting tasteless "pure" protein from it (with the use of artificial flavorings to make the preparations interesting). If the added flavoring is strong enough, it is not necessary for the basic material to be entirely tasteless, as is indicated by the success of "extruded soy protein" in making substitutes for or adding to meat in "sausages," "bacon" strips and "hamburger beef" (Chapter 8).

Leaf Protein

The protein in leaves has long been used by herbivorous animals, which have special adaptations of the gut that enable them to digest the cellulose that is also present. Since human beings are not similarly adapted, attention has instead been given to the possibility of using juices extracted from leaves. Grass juice, for example, expressed by rollers from young grass mowings has been considered. There is much protein in this juice and no indigestible solids. However, its grassy flavor is not appealing to most people. Other sources of leaf protein will be tried; alfalfa, as befits a member of the Leguminosae, gives a huge yield per acre, and is a potential protein source for humans. Brussels sprouts (*Brassica oleracea* var. *gemmifera*) are tightly packed leafy shoot-buds that, as a consequence of their meristematic nature, are rich in proteins. It has been suggested that they represent one of the most economical forms in which leaf protein (for extraction, without the strong brussels sprout flavor) may be grown.

A most interesting situation concerns the relative amounts of protein that can be obtained from the leaves and the grain of maize plants; there is at least as much protein per plant in the leaves (and it has a good amino acid balance) as in the grain. If we were to utilize fully both the leaf protein and the grain of maize plants, we could more than double the yield of protein (and get many times the yield obtained when maize grain alone is fed to domestic animals prior to human consumption).

It is possible that the protein content of various cultivated cereal crop plants could be increased if they could be put into a symbiotic association with nitrogen-fixing bacteria comparable to the association between leguminous plants and *Rhizobium* bacteria. Research is underway on the possibility of encouraging nitrogen-fixing bacteria (*Azotobacter*) to grow in quantity in the immediate vicinity of the roots of cultivated crop grasses. This already occurs in the case of some African range grasses that grow naturally on nitrogen-poor soils. The bacteria obtain their energy from chemicals exuded from the roots of the grasses. Researchers expect to discover the identity of these chemicals and hope to be able to transfer the genes that produce them to the grasses that we call cereals. This may be particularly important now that the shortage and expense of energy cuts down the possibility of making nitrogen-containing fertilizers available in quantity to tropical countries that have "exhausted" soils.

Single Cell Protein

Evidence that a drastic change in our agricultural methods is needed is given by statistics which show that, in 1850, when the world population was approximately one billion, 26 acres of potential crop raising land were available for each person. By 1962, with a world population of three billion, this had shrunk

---

to less than 9 acres; by 2000, it will be down to 4 acres if the population increase continues as expected. Actually, thanks to suburbanization, roadbuilding, and the freezing of land for military purposes (let alone the expansion of recreation and natural preserve areas), it will probably be less. But is there some other way in which we can reap a photosynthetic harvest without the space consuming process of growing flowering plants in soil?

Seventy per cent of the world's surface is covered by the sea. Perhaps greater use can be made of the sunlight that falls on the sea's surface and is available for photosynthesis by small and large marine algae. At any rate, it may well be that algae and other nonflowering plants will come to play a more important role in the human economy. The likeliest candidates are microorganisms; the protein which they produce has come to be categorized as "single cell protein" (even though, strictly speaking, the organisms which produce it are not always unicellular).

Outstanding among the microscopic green algae used in experiments already conducted is the genus *Chlorella*. By varying the conditions under which this unicellular alga is grown, it is possible to vary the proportions of proteins, carbohydrates, and oils produced. Furthermore, because continuous production can be arranged, the yields of protein per acre of culture medium are much higher than could be obtained with any terrestrial crop.

Because *Chlorella* needs to be grown in a liquid (watery) medium with exposure to bright light, we are presented with a paradox. Where there is plenty of water, there is usually a shortage of sunlight, and vice versa. Perhaps when it is possible to convert saltwater to fresh water at a cheap enough rate, the tremendous insolation that the deserts of the world receive can be put to use. Even if this is done, however, there will remain problems in making the resultant products attractive for dietary use. Other algae may be used; one is the blue-green alga *Spirulina*, which is already collected off the mud around Lake Chad in Central Africa and made into edible dried cakes by the inhabitants of the area.

A variation on the original scheme is also being investigated; if it can be made commercially feasible, it will help to solve another of man's growing problems—the most economical disposal of sewage. Scientists at the University of California, Berkeley, have developed a pilot plant for growing microscopic algae and appropriate bacteria together in sewage waste contained in tanks exposed to sunlight. The basis of the process (which supplies algae that can be used as chicken feed) is shown in Fig. 15-1.

The bacteria act on the organic matter, releasing ammonia, which provides the nitrogen nutrition for the algae and their protein-making activities. The oxygen that is released by the algae helps to keep the sewage suspension in a suitable condition for the bacteria to work. The process can operate continuously. In addition to the algal yield, purified water is produced, which may be as important in the future as foodstuff production.

In addition to the use of microscopic algae for the direct production of food, it is to be expected that greater use will be made of the larger algae, particularly seaweeds, as raw material from which chemicals (such as the alginates, which are already important in textile and food-producing industries) and even chemical elements such as iodine may be extracted.

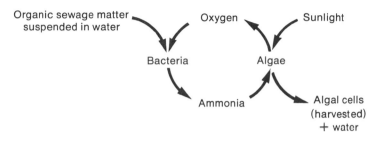

Figure 15-1. Flow chart for the use of microscopic algae in sewage treatment tanks to provide animal feeding-stuffs (algal cells) and reusable water.

So far, we have considered only photosynthetic organisms. Other microorganisms, themselves incapable of photosynthesis, may also have their uses if a source of energy-containing chemicals is at hand (a source which could not be used directly by man). Furthermore, they have divers powers of converting one kind of organic chemical to another, and these may be useful in our quest for more protein. Thus, yeasts which can convert carbohydrates to proteins and vitamins have been used by man since ancient times.

A limited use has already been made of brewers' yeast (*Saccharomyces cereviseae*) left over from the manufacture of beers and wines. If it is not removed from the alcoholic drink, the drinker benefits from both the proteins and the vitamin B content of the yeast itself. Similarly, in bread, where yeast is used in raising the dough, there is dietary value in the yeast that remains in the loaf. However, brewers' yeast is not the richest kind of yeast in protein, and it has a bitter taste. During World War I, research was conducted in Germany on the subject of yeast as a source of food materials, and this research has been continued sporadically. Today, the yeast most used for protein production is a member of another genus, *Candida (Torulopsis) utilis*.

The requirements for growth of this yeast are similar to those of brewers' and bakers' yeasts when these are permitted to grow and multiply at their fastest rate in an aerated medium. After growth, the yeast is filtered off from the liquid medium in which it was suspended. Not only is the dried yeast a rich source of protein (up to 50 per cent), but it also has few equals in its content of the vitamin B-complex, and it has a pleasant flavor. It is now being manufactured in those areas of the world where sugary liquids are available as a raw material. Sugar cane waste, molasses, and the liquors separated from wood pulp in paper-making may all be utilized.

Other fungi than yeasts can convert carbohydrates to proteins, and research is in progress on the possibility of growing them on sweet potatoes, sugar beets, cassava, and other readily produced carbohydrate-rich materials. Research is also being made into the possibility of pretreating the source materials with bacteria and then growing the fungi (including yeasts) on the products of the bacterial action. Bacteria themselves can produce edible protein, and studies are being made on some bacteria which can grow in hydrocarbons (like kerosene) which are by-products of the petroleum industry (although it is to be feared that the oil resources of the world are too limited for this to be a continuing benefit for mankind far into the next century). A potentially more available source of energy for bacteria is methane (CH_4), a constituent of swamp gas that is easily produced from garbage by anaerobic decomposition. A bacterium, *Methanomonas*, grows readily in methane-rich water if given a nitrogen source (e.g., sewage) and a good oxygen supply. It provides a good yield of protein (with a suitable amino acid balance). Once human qualms about ingesting bacterial protein are overcome, it is to be expected that "single cell protein" will become a significant item in our diet.

It is supposed that ultimately our dependence on living organisms for the capture of the sun's energy will be overcome and that artificial—"in vitro"— photosynthesis will become commercially feasible. Also, in time, we shall be able to convert the products of photosynthesis into proteins with as great or greater efficiency than bacteria, plants, and domestic animals. The terrible danger for mankind, however, is that famine, disease, and war will supervene before we attain that chemical ability.

Newly Important Higher Plants

While the search for more rewarding protein sources continues, there are sure to be some important discoveries of special qualities in presently unused or little used plants, especially in the tropics, because the tremendous diversity of plant life there has hardly begun to be analyzed chemically. Unfortunately, tropical forests are being decimated rapidly, and even tropical agriculture is changing in character, so that some of the lesser-known economic plants are in danger of being lost before their qualities are recognized.

One such plant that has elicited enthusiasm is the winged bean (*Psophocarpus tetragonolobus*), a vine native to New Guinea and probably some other areas of southeast Asia (Fig. 15-2). This remarkable leguminous plant produces pods that, when young, make a tender, crunchy vegetable that can be eaten

---

raw or cooked. The pods are rich in proteins, oils, carbohydrates, minerals and vitamins: A, the B group, C, and E. The seeds may be eaten boiled or roasted; the protein in them compares favorably with that of soybeans and complements those of maize and rice, but like soybean protein it is accompanied by a trypsin inhibitor and blood clotting substances (which are removed in the cooking). The seeds are rich in oil (which is 71 per cent unsaturated). This vine also produces root tubers which, unlike most tropical root crops, contain more than 20 per cent protein on a dry weight basis. They can be eaten raw or cooked.

Figure 15-2. *Psophocarpus tetragonolobus:* winged bean. Leaves, inflorescence with pale blue flowers and buds and young and mature pods. The insets on the right are of a cross section of an old pod and seed. Based on a drawing by G. A. C. Herklots. Reproduced by permission.

Finally, the foliage and flowers are also rich in protein and can be eaten raw or cooked by human beings or fed as forage to livestock.

Because the winged bean vine is perennial and bears flowers and fruit over a long season, it is particularly suitable for inclusion in small subsistence farming operations where storage facilities are minimal. Also, because of the activities of the nitrogen-fixing bacteria in its root nodules, it can be used to enrich the soil, especially if it is plowed in as a "green manure." This multipurpose plant has enormous potential for solving many tropical agricultural problems and may become as important in that zone of the world as the soybean is in temperate regions.

Another group of plants that should become increasingly important (if the present enthusiasm for vitamin C-rich diets continues) are those that provide unusually rich supplies of ascorbic acid (vitamin C) in their fruits. Among these is the Chinese gooseberry (*Actinidia chinensis*) of the Actinidiaceae, a dioecious vine from the forests of southern China. This plant bears clusters of brown fruits about the size of lemons. The flesh of the fruit is light green in color and has a delightful taste. Its juice is up to 18 times richer in vitamin C than orange juice, and a single fruit can easily supply a person's normal daily requirement of that vitamin. Although a native of China, *Actinidia* has been cultivated for some time in other countries, particularly New Zealand. Now that the fruits are being imported into the U.S. from New Zealand, they have been named "kiwis," after the flightless bird of those islands. This name has persisted even though they are now cultivated in California.

Another extremely rich source of vitamin C is the "Barbados cherry," (*Malpighia glabra*, Malpighiaceae), a large shrub. Native to the West Indies and the tropical and subtropical areas of the American continental mainland, it produces red, juicy fruits up to an inch in diameter. These fruits have an acid taste, and are most suitable for making preserves and jellies; they are used commercially to boost the vitamin C content of other fruit juices. Some orchards have been set up in Puerto Rico.

The new cereals, the group of triticales (see Chapter 5, page 71), will undoubtedly increase in importance as their superior grain and yield qualities become better known. Also, some new oil plants may be expected to loom larger on the agricultural scene. Thus *Limnanthes* species (Limnanthaceae), with oils that can substitute for sperm whale oil, may become increasingly important.

Another species with considerable economic potential is also of great biological interest because, at least so far, it is chemically unique among the higher plants. This is the jojoba, *Simmondsia chinensis*, which is considered to belong to either the Buxaceae or to a family of its own, the Simmondsiaceae. It is the only flowering plant in which the major non-protein food reserve in the seeds is neither starch nor a fixed oil, but is actually a liquid wax. Waxes differ from oils in that, although they are formed by the combination of fatty acids with an alcohol, the alcohol is a monohydric one rather than the trihydric alcohol glycerol.

To put jojoba in context, it should be pointed out that the present major plant source of wax for polishes and industrial use is the wax palm, *Copernicia cerifera*, a native of northeastern Brazil. This plant produces carnauba wax (the hardest of all waxes, with the highest melting point) as a coating on the epidermis of its leaves. However, the amount of wax produced is so small that no more than six ounces of it may be obtained from 50 of the gigantic leaves of this palm. Although some plantations exist, the tree needs both an area of hot sun and a good water supply at its roots, and is largely restricted to natural drainage basins in Brazil.

Although some other waxes of plant origin are available — for example, from the surface of sugar cane stems (Chapter 7) — there is great need for more of this material. In these circumstances, jojoba has real possibilities. It is a wind-pollinated, dioecious desert shrub from Arizona, California, and adjacent Mexico. Its seeds are about three-quarters of an inch in length and one-third of an inch in diameter; they were used by Indians for food, and the "oil" from them was considered to have medicinal value.

The species was originally described by Link in 1822, from herbarium specimens that were believed to have come from China, and this is the reason for the specific name *chinensis*. It was not until 1933 that the seeds were analyzed chemically; it was then found that 50 per cent of their weight consists of a liquid wax. This wax has many potential uses including the lubrication of high-speed machinery where high temperatures develop. Also it has possibilities of sulfurization for making extreme pressure lubricants. In these uses, jojoba liquid wax is an excellent substitute for sperm whale oil and its availability provides hope that this endangered marine mammal may yet be saved from extinction. Jojoba liquid wax may be hydrogenated into a hard solid wax for the manufacture of polishes, smokeless candles, etc., and, untreated, it can serve as a softening agent for leather and a constituent of chewing gum. It also has cosmetic and pharmaceutic uses.

The presence of this liquid wax in large quantity in the seeds of jojoba presupposes the presence of an enzyme capable of breaking down the wax. If this enzyme can be isolated, it has a number of potential medicinal uses; in particular, it may be possible to utilize it to break down the waxy sheath that surrounds some pathogenic bacteria and protects them from antibiotics.

As this shrub is brought into economical cultivation, it should be particularly successful as a crop plant in those areas where the climate is considered too arid for most other cultivated plants. In view of its first utilization by Native American Indians it will be appropriate if efforts to set up jojoba cultivation and processing as an Indian industry are successful.

Reference was made in Chapter 7 to plants that contain substances that taste sweeter than sugar. Rather different, but biologically extremely interesting, is the so-called "miracle berry"—the fruit of a West African dry forest shrub, *Synsepalum dulcificum* (Sapotaceae). The pulp of these purple berries has only a moderately sweet taste itself, but it causes sour or bland foods to taste sweet. The berries have long been used by West African people to make wine or beer taste sweeter, or simply eaten as an indulgence. Recent research shows that the active principle in the berries is a protein that acts by binding itself to the receptors of the tongue's taste buds so that they signal "sweet" to the brain even though substances that are far from sweet are in the mouth. The protein is now available commercially.

A chemical with similar properties is present in the roots of another West African shrub, *Sphenocentrum jollyanum* (Menispermaceae); the roots themselves have an acid taste. Even the humble artichoke, *Cynara scolymus* (Compositae), has the power to make a glass of water, sipped after eating the vegetable, taste sweet.

Apart from tricks of this sort, drugs of plant origin will continue to be found for testing against human diseases. As an example, alkaloids (vinblastine, etc.) from *Catharanthus roseus* (*Vinca rosea*, Apocynaceae), a small shrub originally from Madagascar but now cultivated widely as an ornamental in tropical regions, hold out promise of value in the treatment of leukemia. There can be little doubt that there are more important drugs still to be found in the tropics. This is recognized by the drug houses, which continue to sponsor exploration in these regions.

Conservation of Agricultural Resources

More efficient utilization of agricultural resources of all sorts is necessary if these resources are to be saved from exhaustion in the face of an increasing human population and its rising expectations. Water supplies will have to be conserved in the drier areas of the world and, in this connection, there will be a greater need of both drought-tolerant plants and cultivated plants capable of growing under irrigation by more saline water than has been used traditionally. Pioneer studies in Israel and India on the use of seawater rather than fresh water for irrigation of selected crops (e.g., sisal, sugar beet and barley) in sandy or gravelly soils have been followed by breeding experiments at the University of California, Davis, on the selection of barley strains capable of yielding well under these same circumstances. Needless to say, there are still problems connected with the transportation of even saline water to all areas where the soil is appropriate for such farming, and the possible danger to freshwater supplies from an accumulation of salts underground also has to be considered.

Soil conservation of a sort has been practiced by inhabitants of tropical forest regions by "shifting cultivation" methods, in which an area of forest is cut (and usually burned) and used to raise crops for a few years until its soil nutrients are depleted. Then the forest is allowed to take over and re-establish a tree cover, and the soil gradually recovers its former nutrient status. Only after a couple of decades or more have passed is the forest cleared again. However, increasing human populations in these regions are seriously reducing the number of years that can be allowed to go by before the forest is cut and used again, and soil fertility is not allowed to recover fully. Because importation of fertilizers into these regions is out of the question economically, the solution to this problem must come from agriculture which mimics natural ecosystems more completely. Thus, in Samoa, an experiment in imitating the layering of a natural forest has been initiated, with coconut palms representing the trees, cacao trees, the understorey, and taro, the herb layer. Soil qualities are preserved in such a set-up.

Where the removal of crop plants is a necessary part of harvesting the crop, it will become increasingly important to see that the "wastes" are returned to the soil in decomposed or decomposable form (compost). The principles of "organic" gardening and farming are ecologically sound and will certainly be followed more and more as manufactured fertilizers become scarcer and more expensive. Agriculture may see a return to multi-purpose plants (such as the winged bean, *Psophocarpus,* described earlier) and a multi-purpose use of present "specialty" plants (such as maize and sugar cane). If this seems to be "where we came in" (Chapter 1), it is no coincidence; we face problems of limited resources that are different from those of the agricultural pioneers, but no less severe.

Conservation of Natural Resources

It is by applying ecological principles to agriculture that the close link between plants and human beings will be perpetuated. There is, however, another aspect of the relationship that we must learn to appreciate before the future can be regarded with confidence, and this is the conservation of natural vegetational resources. Although regard for their recreational and esthetic values is increasing, the great stretches of natural and semi-natural vegetation in the world are being destroyed at a prodigious rate. Contributing to this are urbanization, utilization without replacement, and sheer irresponsibility in the starting of fires and the promotion of erosion, as well as the importation of potential animal and plant pests from other regions. Tropical forests in particular are being destroyed—their conversion to cattle pastures is the least ecologically disastrous result but, all too often, a wasteland is created. There is accelerating pollution of all parts of the environment by the chemical products we have learned how to make but not how to use efficiently and for whose disposal we have only the most rudimentary ideas.

Human beings, who through their intellectual and social evolution have reached a position from which they can expect to control the utilization of every square foot of this planet (and possibly others besides), may still destroy themselves and everything around them if they seek only short-term gains from their enormous technological capabilities. To save themselves, and the other inhabitants of the earth, human beings must pay increasing attention to ecological principles; they must learn the laws that govern the relations between organisms and their environments. And knowledge of these laws will not be enough; there must be an increased awareness of the facts of mankind's relationship with nature—the facts as they were, as they are, and as they could be in the future. This is the reason for writing and reading about *Plants and Civilization*. Perhaps this book will help a little in bringing about such an awareness.

Suggestions for Further Reading

Amerine, M. A., and V. L. Singleton. *Wine: An Introduction for Americans.* Berkeley: University of California Press, 1968.

Anderson, E. *Man and Life,* 2nd ed. Berkeley: University of California Press, 1969.

Angier, B. *Field Guide to Edible Wild Plants.* Harrisburg, Pa.: Stackpole Books, 1974.

Arber, A. *Herbals,* 2nd ed. Cambridge, England: Cambridge University Press, 1953.

Bailey, L. H. *Manual of Cultivated Plants,* revised ed. New York: The Macmillan Co., 1949.

Baker, H. G. "Human Influences on Plant Evolution." *Economic Botany,* Vol. 26, pp. 32–43, 1972.

Barnes, A. C. *The Sugar Cane.* London: Leonard Hill (New York: Interscience), 1964.

Bolton, J. L. *Alfalfa: Botany, Cultivation* and *Utilization.* London: Leonard Hill (New York: Interscience), 1962.

Brown, L. R. *Seeds of Change: The Green Revolution and Development in the 1970's.* New York: Praeger, 1970.

Christensen, C. M. *The Molds and Man: An Introduction to the Fungi.* Minneapolis: University of Minnesota Press, 1951.

Coon, C. S. *The Story of Man.* New York: Alfred A. Knopf, 1954.

Coon, N. *The Dictionary of Useful Plants.* Emmaus, Pa: Rodale Press, 1974.

de Candolle, A. L. P. P. *Origins of Cultivated Plants* (reprinted from the 1884 edition in the International Science Series). New York: Hafner, 1963.

Deerr, N. *The History of Sugar,* 2 vols. London: Chapman and Hall, 1949–50.

Dodd, A. P. *The Biological Campaign against Prickly-Pear.* Brisbane, Australia: Commonwealth Prickly Pear Board, 1940.

Economic Botany, quarterly journal. The Society for Economic Botany, New York Botanical Garden, New York.

Ehrlich, P. R. *The Population Bomb.* New York: Ballantine Books, 1968.

Emboden, W. A., Jr. *Narcotic Plants.* New York: Macmillan, 1972.

Food and Agriculture. A Scientific American Book. San Francisco: W. H. Freeman & Co., 1976.

Frankel, O. H., and E. Bennett, eds. *Genetic Resources in Plants — Their Exploration and Conservation.* Oxford: Blackwell (Philadelphia: F. A. Davis), 1970.

Frankel, O. H., and J. G. Hawkes, eds. *Crop Genetic Resources for Today and Tomorrow.* New York: Cambridge University Press, 1975.

Galinat, W. C. "The Evolutionary Emergence of Maize." *Bulletin of the Torrey Botanical Club,* Vol. 102, pp. 313–324, 1975.

Galinat, W. C. "The Origin of Maize." *Annual Review of Genetics,* Vol. 5, pp. 447–478, 1971.

Greenland, D. J. "Bringing the Green Revolution to the Shifting Cultivator." *Science,* Vol. 190, pp. 841–844, 1975.

Grist, D. H. *Rice.* London: Longmans, Green & Co., 1953.

Harlan, J. R. *Crops and Man.* Madison, Wisc.: American Society of Agronomy: Crop Science Society of America, 1975.

Heiser, C. B., Jr. *Nightshades, the Paradoxical Plants.* San Francisco: W. H. Freeman, 1964.

Heiser, C. B. Jr. *Seed to Civilization.* San Francisco: W. H. Freeman, 1973.

Herklots, G. A. C. *Vegetables in Southeast Asia.* London: Allen and Unwin, 1972.

Heyerdahl, T. *American Indians in the Pacific: The Theory behind the Kon-Tiki Expedition.* London: Allen and Unwin, 1952.

Hurry, J. B. *The Woad Plant and Its Dye.* London: Oxford University Press, 1930.

Hutchinson, J. B., R. A. Silow, and S. G. Stephens. *The Evolution of Gossypium and the Differentiation of Cultivated Cottons.* London: Oxford University Press, 1947.

Janick, J., R. W. Schery, F. W. Woods, and V. W. Ruttan. *Plant Science, An Introduction to World Crops.* San Francisco: W. H. Freeman, 1969.

Kierstead, S. P. *Natural Dyes.* Boston: Bruce Humphries, 1950.

Kirby, R. H. *Vegetable Fibres; Botany, Cultivation, and Utilization.* London: Leonard Hill (New York: Interscience), 1963.

Kreig, M. B. *Green Medicine: The Search for Plants That Heal.* Chicago: Rand, McNally and Co., 1964.

Lappe, F. M. *Diet for a Small Planet.* New York: Ballantine Books, 1971.

Lewis, W. H., and M. P. F. Elvin-Lewis, *Medical Botany.* Somerset, N. J.: Wiley-Interscience, 1977.

Mangelsdorf, P. C. *Corn, Its Origin, Evolution and Improvement.* Cambridge, Mass.: Harvard University Press, 1974.

Mangelsdorf, P. C., R. S. MacNeish, and G. R. Willey. "Origins of Agriculture in Middle America." In *Handbook of Middle American Indians,* Vol. 1. Austin: University of Texas Press, 1965.

Masefield, G. B., M. Wallis, S. G. Harrison, and B. E. Nicholson. *The Oxford Book of Food Plants.* London: Oxford University Press, 1969.

Merrill, E. D. *The Botany of Cook's Voyages.* Waltham, Mass: Chronica Botanica Co., 1954.

Mors, W. B., and C. T. Rizzini. *Useful Plants of Brazil.* San Francisco: Holden-Day, 1966.

National Academy of Sciences. *Guayule.* Washington, D.C., 1977.

National Academy of Sciences. *Underexploited Tropical Plants with Promising Economic Value.* Washington, D.C., 1975.

National Academy of Sciences. *The Winged Bean: A High Protein Crop for the Tropics.* Washington, D.C., 1975.

Norman, A. G. *The Soybean — Genetics, Breeding, Physiology, Nutrition, Management.* New York: Academic Press. 1963.

Ochse, J. J., M. J. Soule, M. J. Dijkman, and C. Wehlberg. *Tropical and Subtropical Agriculture,* 2 vols. New York: Macmillan, 1961.

Parry, J. W. *Spices,* 2nd. ed. New York: Chemical Publishing Co., 1972.

Peterson, R. F. *Wheat: Botany, Cultivation and Utilization.* London: Leonard Hill (New York: Interscience), 1965.

Pirie, N. W. *Food Resources: Conventional and Novel.* Baltimore: Penguin Books, 1969.

Polhamus, L. G. *Rubber: Botany, Production and Utilization.* London: Leonard Hill (New York: Interscience), 1962.

Purseglove, J. W. *Tropical Crops — Dicotyledons,* 2 vols. London: Longmans, Green & Co. (New York: John Wiley), 1968.

Purseglove, J. W. *Tropical Crops — Monocotyledons,* 2 vols. London: Longmans, Green & Co. (New York: Halstead Press), 1972.

Renfrew, J. M. *Palaeoethnobotany.* London: Methuen & Co., 1973.

Riley, C. L., J. C. Kelley, C. W. Pennington, and R. L. Rands, eds. *Man across the Sea: Problems of Pre-Columbian Contacts.* Austin: University of Texas Press, 1971.

Rosengarten, F., Jr. *The Book of Spices.* Philadelphia: Livingston Publishing Co., 1969.

Salaman, R. N. *The History and Social Influence of the Potato.* Cambridge, England: Cambridge University Press, 1949.

Sauer, C. O. *Agricultural Origins and Dispersals.* New York: American Geographical Society, 1952.

Schery, R. W. *Plants for Man,* 2nd ed. Englewood Cliffs, N.J.: Prentice-Hall, 1972.

Schultes, R. E. *Hallucinogenic Plants, A Golden Guide*. New York: Golden Press, 1976.

Schultes, R. E. "Hallucinogens of Plant Origin." *Science*, Vol. 163, pp. 245–254, 1969.

Schwanitz, F. *The Origin of Cultivated Plants*. Cambridge, Mass.: Harvard University Press, 1966.

Scott, J. M. *The Great Tea Venture*. New York: E. P. Dutton and Co., 1965.

Simmonds, N. W. *Bananas*. London: Longmans, 1969.

Simmonds, N. W., ed. *Evolution of Crop Plants*. London: Longmans, 1976.

Singer, R. *Mushrooms and Truffles: Botany, Cultivation and Utilization*. London: Leonard Hill (New York: Interscience), 1961.

Stakman, E. C., E. R. Bradfield, and P. C. Mangelsdorf. *Campaigns against Hunger*. Cambridge, Mass.: Belknap Press of Harvard University Press, 1967.

Swain, T., ed. *Plants in the Development of Modern Medicine*. Cambridge, Mass.: Harvard University Press, 1972.

Thompson, C. J. S. *The Mystic Mandrake*. London: Rider & Co., 1934.

Tippo, O., and W. L. Stern. *Humanistic Botany*. New York: W. W. Norton & Co., 1977.

Towle, M. A. *The Ethnobotany of Pre-Columbian Peru*. Chicago: Aldine Publishing Co., 1961.

Tsoumis, G. *Wood As a Raw Material*. Elmsford, N.Y.: Pergamon Press, 1968.

Ucko, P. J., and D. W. Dimbleby, eds. *The Domestication and Exploitation of Plants and Animals*. Chicago: Aldine Publishing Co., 1969.

Uphof, J. C. T. *Dictionary of Economic Plants*, 2nd ed. Würzburg, Germany: Cramer (New York: Stechert-Hafner), 1968.

Urquhart, D. H. *Cocoa*, 2nd ed. New York: John Wiley, 1961.

Vavilov, N. I. *The Origin, Variation, Immunity and Breeding of Cultivated Plants*. Selected writings translated from the Russian by K. S. Chester. Waltham, Mass.: Chronica Botanica Co., 1951.

Weiss, E. A. *Castor, Sesame and Safflower*. London: Leonard Hill (New York: Interscience), 1971.

Wellman, F. L. *Coffee: Botany, Cultivation and Utilization*. London: Leonard Hill (New York: Interscience), 1962.

Whitaker, T. W., and G. N. Davis. *Cucurbits: Botany, Cultivation, Utilization*. London: Leonard Hill (New York: Interscience), 1962.

Wilson, C. M. *Grass and People*. Gainesville: University of Florida Press, 1961.

Wyman, D. *The Arboretums and Botanical Gardens of North America*. Waltham, Mass.: Chronica Botanica Co., 1947.

Yen, D. E. *The Sweet Potato and Oceania*. B. P. Bishop Museum Bulletin 236, Honolulu, 1963.

Index
